C000050968

The Complete

IDIOT'S

Guide to

QBasic™

by Greg Perry

a

alpha
books

A Division of Macmillan Computer Publishing
201 West 103rd Street, Indianapolis, Indiana 46290 USA

For Jerry Pournelle, whose stories I read and whose articles I always agree with.

©1994 Alpha Books

International Standard Book Number: 1-56761-490-6
Library of Congress Catalog Card Number: 94-70616

96 95 94   9 8 7 6 5 4 3 2 1

Interpretation of the printing code: the rightmost number of the second series of numbers is the number of the book's printing. For example, a printing code of 94-1 shows that the first printing of the book occurred in 1994.

Printed in the United States of America

Publisher
Richard K. Swadley

Associate Publisher
Jordan Gold

Acquisitions Manager
Stacey Hiquet

Development Editor
Dean Miller

Senior Editor
Tad Ringo

Production Editor
Cheri Clark

Editorial Coordinator
Bill Whitmer

Editorial Assistant
Sharon Cox

Technical Reviewer
Keith Davenport

Cover Designer
Scott Cook

Designers
Amy Peppler-Adams, Barbara Webster

Illustrations
Steve Vanderbosch

Indexer
Jeanne Clark

Production Team
Gary Adair, Brad Chinn, Kim Cofer, Meshell Dinn, Marc Enochs, Stephanie Gregory, Jenny Kucera, Beth Rago, Marc Shecter, Kris Simmons, Greg Simsic, Carol Stamile, Robert Wolf

About the Author

Greg Perry is a speaker and writer in both the programming and the applications side of computing. He is known for bringing programming topics down to the beginner's level. Perry has been a programmer and trainer for the past 15 years. He received his first degree in computer science, and then he received a master's degree in corporate finance. Besides writing, he teaches, consults, and lectures across the country, including at the acclaimed Software Development programming conferences. Perry is the author of 18 other computer books, including *Absolute Beginner's Guide to Programming, Absolute Beginner's Guide to C, Turbo C++ Programming 101, Moving from C and C++*, and *QBasic Programming 101* (all published by Sams Publishing). In addition, he has published articles in several publications, such as *PC World, Data Training*, and *Inside First Publisher*. In his spare time, he gives lectures on traveling in Italy, his second-favorite place to be.

Acknowledgments

I want to thank Dean Miller, who edits with style, Keith Davenport, who edits with accuracy, and Cheri Clark, who edits with grace. They made this book into what I could not.

Stacy Hiquet, Jordan Gold, and Richard Swadley continue to ask me back to Sams Publishing, and I am so very grateful that they do. I hope my sluggish writing speeds and my inability to tackle a wide range of writing subjects don't turn them off too much.

In the end, my beautiful bride, Jayne, and my parents, Glen and Bettye, keep me going.

Contents at a Glance

Contents at a Glance

This page unintentionally left blank.

Contents

Here's that blank page thing again.

Introduction

Do you think you'll *never* be able to program computers? Would you like to learn QBasic but just don't have the time or energy? Is your old, worn-out computer in need of new programs to spice up its circuits? This book is just what the doctor ordered!

The Complete Idiot's Guide to QBasic breaks the commonality of computer books by talking directly at your level while not talking down to you. *The Complete Idiot's Guide to QBasic* is like your best friend sitting next to you teaching QBasic. This book attempts to *express* without having to *impress*. *The Complete Idiot's Guide to QBasic* talks to you in plain language, not in computerese. This book, with its short chapters, line drawings, and often-humorous straight talk, makes your trip through the maze of QBasic programming faster and friendlier, and easier than in any other book available today.

Who Is This Book For?

This is a beginner's book. If you have never programmed before, this book is for you. No knowledge of any programming concept is assumed. If you can't even spell *PC*, you can learn to program QBasic with this book.

The term beginner has different meanings at different times. You might be new to computers. You might never have programmed before. You might have programmed in other languages, but are a beginner to QBasic. In any case, read on, faithful one, because in 29 quick chapters, you'll know QBasic.

What Makes This Book Different?

This book does not cloud issues with internal technical stuff that beginners to QBasic programming don't need. I, your author, am of the firm belief that introductory principles have to be taught well and slowly. After the basics are tackled, the "harder" parts never seem hard. This book teaches you the real QBasic that you need to get started.

QBasic was designed for beginners. If QBasic is the first language you have decided to learn, you picked a winner. QBasic is kind to beginners, while providing the commands needed by the experts.

Any subject, whether it be brain surgery, mail sorting, or QBasic programming, is easy if explained properly. Nobody can teach you anything, because you have to teach yourself. But if the instructor, book, or video doing the teaching doesn't make the subject simple and fun, you won't *want* to learn the subject.

I challenge you to find a more straightforward approach to QBasic than is offered in *The Complete Idiot's Guide to QBasic*. If you can, call me, because I'd like to read it too (you thought maybe I'd offer your money back?). Seriously, I have attempted to provide you with a different kind of help from that which you find in most other places.

The biggest advantage *The Complete Idiot's Guide to QBasic* offers is that the author (still me) really *likes* QBasic. Unlike most "computer people," I learned to write BASIC programs (BASIC is the predecessor of QBasic) before I learned anything else. When I first sat down at a computer years ago, it was in front of a BASIC language manual, and I've been hooked ever since. I hope I can help to hook you also.

Conventions Used in This Book

The following conventions are used in this book:

- ☞ Code lines, variables, any text you see on-screen and parts of the program output that the user typed are in **bold monospace**.

- ☞ Placeholders on format lines are in *italic monospace*.

- ☞ Filenames are in regular text, all uppercase (for example, SLOTS.BAS).

- ☞ Optional parameters in syntax explanations are enclosed in flat brackets ([]). You do *not* type the brackets when you include these parameters.

☛ New terms appear in *italic*.

☛ Some code lines are too long to fit on a single line in the book. A line with the code-continuation character, ➥, has been continued from the preceding line.

Index to the Icons and Boxes

Like many computer books, this book contains lots of helpful hints, tips, and warnings. You will run across many *icons* (little pictures) and various shaded boxes that bring these items to your attention. A glance at an icon gives you a quick idea of the purpose of the text next to the icon (or in the shaded box).

Here are descriptions of the icons and boxes:

This icon points out potential problems you could face with a particular topic being discussed. Often, the icon indicates a warning that you should heed, or it provides a way to fix a problem that can occur.

All of this book's hints and tips (and there are lots of them) are highlighted by this icon. When a really neat feature or code trick coincides with the topic you are reading about, this icon pinpoints just what you can do to take advantage of the bonus.

Throughout the QBasic language, there are subjects that provide a deeper level of understanding than others. These boxes let you know about something you might not have thought about, such as a new use for the topic being discussed.

TECHNO NERD TEACHES...

If you don't want anything more than the beginning essentials of QBasic, don't read the material next to this icon. Actually, most of you will enjoy this material, but be aware that you can safely skip it without losing the meaning of the chapter.

How Can I Have Fun With QBasic?

Chapter 29 contains a complete, working slot-machine program. The program was kept as short as possible without sacrificing readable code and game-playing functionality. After you learn QBasic, you'll easily be able to access QBasic's specific graphics, sound, and input routines to improve the program.

The program uses as much of this book's content as possible. Almost every topic taught in the book appears in the slot-machine game. Too many books offer nothing more than snippets of code. The slot-machine game in this book gives you a chance to see the *big picture*. As you progress through the book, you'll understand more and more of the game.

What Do I Do Now?

Turn the page and learn the QBasic language.

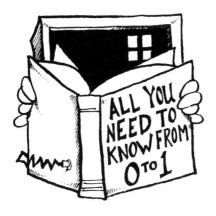

Chapter 1

What Is QBasic? A Fun Programming Language

In This Chapter

- ☛ What is a program?
- ☛ What you need in order to write QBasic programs
- ☛ The programming process

Welcome to the world of QBasic programming! This book will be your guide on the tour through introductory programming. This book shows you that anyone can program computers because programming computers is fun and easy. The programming field seems to never have enough programmers to fill the demand for the programs that have to be written. The tremendous growth in programming jobs seems to have no end in sight. More and more people and businesses are using computers every day.

If you have never written a program in your life, don't worry. This chapter begins at the beginning, teaching you introductory programming concepts, explaining what a program is, and reviewing a short history of the QBasic language. Get ready to be excited! QBasic is a programming language rich in capabilities but easy to master.

What Is a Program?

A computer is nothing more than a dumb machine waiting around for you to give it instructions. When you use a word processor or a spreadsheet, your computer doesn't really know what it's doing. The computer blindly follows instructions without getting bored. Computers do not think or make decisions on their own. Computers must be given extremely detailed instructions before they do anything.

SPEAK LIKE A GEEK

Without **programs**, the computer would just sit idle, not knowing what to do next. A word processing program contains a list of detailed instructions, written in a computer language such as QBasic, that tells the computer exactly how to be a word processor. When you **run** a program, you are telling the computer to follow the instructions in the program that you have supplied.

You must supply the detailed instructions when you want your computer to perform a specific task. Those instructions are known as *programs*. A program contains lines of *code,* or instructions that the computer understands. If computers understood English or another spoken language, people wouldn't have to learn to program! Computers cannot, however, understand spoken language. We must meet the computer halfway by supplying instructions in a programming language such as QBasic. The computer then takes those QBasic instructions and translates them into an internal format that is understood by the computer.

There are thousands of programs you can buy for your computer, but when a business wants a computer to perform a specific task, the business hires programmers to write programs that follow needed specifications. You will find uses for your computer, but there may not be a program on the market that does what you really want. This book rescues you from that dilemma. After you learn QBasic, you will be able to write programs that contain instructions which tell the computer how to behave.

A computer program tells your computer how to do what you want. Just as a chef needs a recipe to make a dish, a computer needs instructions to produce results. A recipe is nothing more than a set of detailed instructions that, if properly written, describe the steps needed to prepare a food item. That is exactly what a computer program is to your computer.

Programs produce *output* when you *run* or *execute* them. The cooked dish is a recipe's *output,* and the payroll or word processor is the output produced by a running program. If no output were needed, there would be no need for computers or computer programs. Your computer exists to perform tasks and create output that you need.

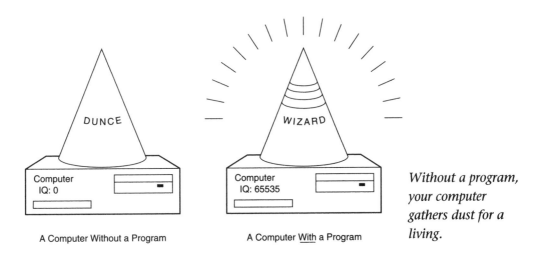

DUNCE

Computer
IQ: 0

A Computer Without a Program

WIZARD

Computer
IQ: 65535

A Computer With a Program

Without a program, your computer gathers dust for a living.

What You Need in Order to Write QBasic Programs

If you are unfamiliar with DOS, have no fear! You don't have to be a DOS wizard to use QBasic.

Before you can write and execute a QBasic program on your computer, you need a QBasic *programming language*. The QBasic programming language, more accurately known by the computer industry as a QBasic *interpreter*, takes the QBasic program you write, interprets it (which is a technical term for making the program computer-readable), and then runs the program so that you can look at the resulting output. Today's QBasic interpreter is much more advanced than the predecessor BASIC language interpreters of a few years ago.

The QBasic interpreter is supplied free with each version of DOS sold today. Starting with DOS 5.0, Microsoft Corporation (the founding company of QBasic and many other versions of BASIC over the years) wants to provide everybody with the QBasic language so that today's beginners will have a head start toward becoming tomorrow's expert programmers.

Microsoft Corporation has been writing versions of the BASIC language for almost 20 years now. In one of the earliest renditions, called *MBASIC* (for *Microsoft BASIC*), Microsoft took a language written for beginners and added powerful features while maintaining the ease of use that beginners need. Over the years, Microsoft made many refinements to BASIC. The result is QBasic, one of the most powerful interpreted languages on the market today, and still one of the cheapest (free!).

Don't let that long acronym dissuade you! QBasic is easier to use than its silver-dollar abbreviation would lead you to believe. The key word is *Beginner's*.

BASIC began as an alternative to the harder-to-use FORTRAN programming language. Nonprogramming students who needed to write programs for their classes didn't need to fight both their own subject material and a difficult programming language. Therefore some college professors put their heads together and developed BASIC, which stands for *Beginner's All-Purpose Symbolic Instruction Code*.

Microsoft Corporation offers other versions of BASIC, the most notable one being the QuickBASIC *compiler* and Visual BASIC for Windows. (A compiler is a lot like an interpreter, but is a little more trouble to use.) Microsoft's Word for Windows word processor and Microsoft Access (a powerful database system) include BASIC-like languages as well. When you master QBasic, you'll be more than ready to tackle these other versions of BASIC.

The Programming Process

Most people follow these basic steps when writing any program:

1. Decide exactly what the program is to do.

2. Use an *editor* to write and save the programming language instructions. An editor is a lot like a word processor (although not usually as fancy) that enables you to create and edit text. All QBasic program filenames end in .BAS.

3. Run the program.

4. Check for program errors. If there are any, fix them and go back to step 3.

TECHNO NERD TEACHES...

The QBasic program you write is called *source code.* The QBasic interpreter takes QBasic source code and translates the code into *machine language.* Computers are made up of nothing more than thousands of electrical switches that are either *on* or *off.* Computers must ultimately be given instructions in *binary.* The prefix *bi* means two, and the two states of electricity are called *binary states.* It's a lot easier to use the QBasic interpreter to convert your QBasic programs into 1s and 0s that represent internal on-and-off switch settings than for you to do it yourself.

QBasic enables you to perform these steps easily, all from within the same environment. For instance, you can use QBasic's editor to enter a program, run the program, view any errors, fix the errors, run the program, and look at the results, all from within the same screen and using a uniform set of menus.

If you have never programmed before, this all might seem confusing. Relax. This book will hold your hand the entire way, and challenge you to learn at the same time.

An error in a computer program is called a **bug**. Getting rid of errors is called **debugging** a program. Many times, QBasic finds bugs in your programs. If you spell a command incorrectly, for instance, QBasic tells you so when you attempt to run the program. The first bug really was a bug! A moth was lodged in an early printer, which lead to the term computer bug.

In a nutshell, you really have to take only these steps when writing QBasic programs: Start QBasic, type your program, and press **Shift+F5** (one of the keyboard's *function keys*) to run your program. QBasic takes care of interpreting and executing the program.

Put on your thinking caps and set your phasers on "QBasic," because the next chapter takes you on a journey through the QBasic environment.

The Least You Need to Know

☞ Make sure you have a version of DOS that is 5.0 or later.

☞ Learn the QBasic programming language. This book takes care of that!

☞ Don't get nervous, because QBasic programs are easy to write. The QBasic environment has many more features than you will ever have to learn.

Chapter 2

How Do I Use QBasic? Learn the QBasic Editor

In This Chapter

- Starting QBasic
- Looking at QBasic's environment
- QBasic to the rescue
- Saving your work
- Loading your work
- Quitting QBasic

This chapter puts you at ease inside QBasic's environment. You won't learn how to write QBasic programs yet—that begins in the next chapter. You will see here how to start QBasic, and how to load programs from (and save programs to) the disk.

You cannot physically harm your computer from its keyboard (you can only hurt its feelings—just kidding). Therefore, after you load QBasic, play around and try a few things. The only way to learn something like QBasic is to use it.

Starting QBasic

Hopefully your computer has a hard disk. If it does not, the way you start QBasic will be different from the method described here. Even some readers who have hard disks will have trouble loading QBasic because of a nonstandard method that was used to load QBasic and DOS originally. If you have problems, this is one of the few times you'll have to learn a little about DOS (or, better yet, ask a friend to help you). Most readers of this book will be able to start QBasic by following these steps:

1. Turn on the computer if it is not already on.

2. Find the *DOS prompt*, which usually looks like this:

   C:\>

   If you see a letter other than C before the :\>, that means that a drive other than C is currently active. Do not worry if C is not the active drive; things should still work fine.

3. Type **QBASIC** at the DOS prompt. Press **Esc** (Escape) to get rid of the copyright message box, and you'll see the screen shown in the figure (which also points out a few areas of the screen that we'll need to discuss in this chapter).

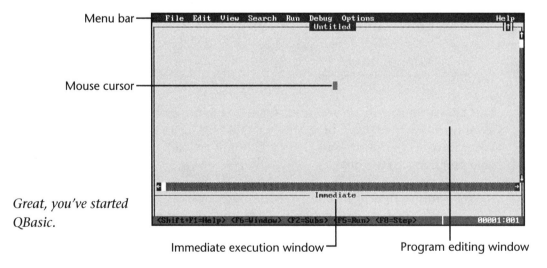

Menu bar

Mouse cursor

Great, you've started QBasic.

Immediate execution window

Program editing window

Looking at QBasic's Environment

The large blank area in the middle of the screen is called the *program editing window*. Here you will see your program as you type it, just as you see your text on a word processor's screen as you enter text there.

If you are running QBasic from Windows, double-click on the **QBasic** icon in the Main Program Group.

The *text cursor* marks the location of the current character. As you type, the cursor moves forward. As you edit text, you can move the text cursor up, down, left, and right to change your editing position. If you have a mouse, you will see the *mouse cursor* as well. The mouse cursor enables you to move the text cursor quickly. Instead of using the arrow keys, you can move the mouse cursor and click the left mouse button, and the text cursor will move to wherever the mouse cursor is at the time.

The mouse cursor is useful for selecting, cutting, and pasting blocks of text. You can also use the mouse cursor to click within the horizontal and vertical scroll bars to scroll the screen over different parts of a long program. And you can use the mouse cursor to select from QBasic's wide assortment of menus, which are discussed in a moment.

The status line in the lower right corner of the screen shows the line and column of the text cursor's current position. (The *line number* is the five-digit number to the left of the colon; the *column number* is to the right of the colon.)

Type a few things into QBasic's editing window, and watch the screen as you do so. The line and column numbers will change as you type, and the text cursor will move too. If you have a mouse, move it around and click it a few times as well.

If QBasic displays an error message as you type, press **Enter** to get rid of the error. For now, it is important that you get familiar with QBasic's editor so you can give your full concentration to the language later.

TECHNO NERD TEACHES...

The *immediate execution window* is handy if you want to try a one-line QBasic statement. You can move the cursor down to this area and type a line of code such as **PRINT 20*30** to see the results immediately. The line you type here does not affect the program in the editing window above.

SPEAK LIKE A GEEK

A **menu** is a list of options displaying the orders you can issue to QBasic.

QBasic includes a *menu bar* across the top of the screen, with options such as File, Edit, and View. You can select from any of the menus in one of two ways:

☞ Press the **Alt** key, then press the boldfaced letter of the menu option you want to choose.

☞ If you have a mouse, move the mouse pointer over the option, and click the left mouse button.

SPEAK LIKE A GEEK

The menu you see when you select from the menu bar is called a **pull-down menu** because the menu acts like a rolling window shade that you might pull down.

Choose any of the pull-down menu options by moving the highlight bar over the option with the arrow keys and pressing **Enter**. You can use the mouse to choose an option by moving the mouse cursor so that it points to the option, and then clicking the left mouse button.

Display a menu option by selecting File. QBasic displays a list of items under File from which you can choose by pressing the **arrow** keys and **Enter**, or by clicking with the mouse.

The tear-out card in this book contains a description of QBasic's menu options. Beginning QBasic programmers have little use for most of the menu options on the various pull-down menus.

As you glance through the QBasic pull-down menus, you will notice that some options have keystrokes listed next to them. For instance, the Start option on the Run pull-down menu has "Shift+F5" listed next to it. Shift+F5 is the *shortcut key* for that option; instead of selecting the option from the menu, you need only press **Shift+F5** and QBasic will know that you want to select **Start** from the **Run** pull-down menu. Pressing Shift+F5 is quicker than selecting from the menu.

Most of the shortcut keys use one of the function keys listed on the side or across the top of your keyboard (the keys labeled F1 through F10 or F12). This book's tear-out card lists all the QBasic shortcut keys.

Do not try to memorize the shortcut keys now—rely on the menus to tell you what you can do next. As you use QBasic, you will learn the shortcut keys.

Using the shortcut keys is quicker than selecting from the menus, even if you have a mouse. Nevertheless, these keys take some time to learn. As you use QBasic's menus, pay attention to the shortcut keys, and learn the ones for the menu options you use most.

Some of the menu options have an ellipsis after them, such as the **Display...** option from the **Options** menu. Instead of performing an action, these menu options produce dialog boxes. Often, a dialog box requires that you type a program filename to load or save, as the section "Loading Your Work" shows you later in this chapter.

QBasic to the Rescue

When you really need help with QBasic, ask QBasic! QBasic supplies lots of helpful advice you can use for editing and programming. Although QBasic supplies several kinds of help, most of the time you'll want help with a particular command.

A **dialog box** appears when QBasic needs more information to carry out your command.

Pull down the **Help** menu, and look through some of the other kinds of help that QBasic provides. The right mouse button brings up help also.

For instance, type **PRINT** in the QBasic editing window, and then press **F1** (the help shortcut key). QBasic displays a large help screen in place of the editing window, describing the ins and outs of the **PRINT** command. Pressing **Esc** gets rid of the help screen. The F1 key produces *context-sensitive help*, which is a fancy term meaning that you get help on the command at the cursor's current location.

Notice that QBasic restores your editing window when you are through viewing the help screen.

Saving Your Work

Save your QBasic program to disk often. If the power goes out (or more likely, some goof walks along and pulls out your power cord from the wall), you will lose any work you haven't saved to disk. Type something into your QBasic editing window (it doesn't have to be an actual program), and select **S**ave from the File pull-down menu. Type a filename next to the File Name prompt. If you try to leave QBasic before saving your file, QBasic warns you, and gives you one last chance to save your program.If you understand DOS drive and subdirectory names, you can type either one before the filename.

The filename must be a valid one-to-eight-character DOS filename. All QBasic program files should end in the .BAS filename extension. You don't have to type the .BAS extension because QBasic supplies that for you.

Loading Your Work

If you want to load a program from disk into memory, you can do so through the File pull-down menu. Before loading the program you just saved, select File New. This action erases your program editing window and prepares QBasic for a new program file. (If you don't select File New, QBasic will replace whatever is in the editing window with the loaded file anyway.)

Select File **O**pen from the pull-down menus. Type the filename you entered in the preceding section. Again, you don't have to type the .BAS extension; QBasic assumes that all your QBasic program files end in .BAS. (You can also just select the file from the list of filenames.) You will see the text you entered at the end of the preceding section.

You can load only one file at a time into QBasic. If you want to change two or more QBasic programs, you'll have to load and change them one at a time.

Quitting QBasic

Before you return to the operating system, save your work if you haven't already, and then select File Exit from the pull-down menus. QBasic closes up, and you return to DOS.

The Least You Need to Know

☞ Start QBasic and practice entering text.

☞ Always save your program to disk so that it will be there the next time you want to work on it.

☞ Remember the F1 help key because QBasic's help is there when you need it.

☞ Don't use a strange filename extension. QBasic expects the .BAS filename extension on all your program files.

Recycling tip:
tear this page out and photocopy it.

Chapter 3

What's a QBasic Program Like? The Program's Format

In This Chapter

- ☛ The forest without the trees
- ☛ Looking at a longer program
- ☛ Scanning a long program
- ☛ Printing a program listing

This chapter eases you into QBasic by getting you used to the *big picture*. Before you are done, you'll be able to recognize a QBasic program and understand what is needed to run one. You learned in the preceding chapter that entering a QBasic program takes no more effort than entering text into a word processor. A program is nothing more than lines of instructions that you type. Many of QBasic's commands look just like their English equivalents, such as **PRINT**, **IF**, and **WHILE**.

A complete QBasic program follows this paragraph. The program is short; QBasic programs don't have to be mammoth to be useful. Glance through the code. At this point, you don't have to understand any of the individual lines. Familiarize yourself with the program's look and feel.

```
REM Introductory program
REM This program prints your name across the screen.
CLS
INPUT "What is your first name"; firstName$
```

```
CLS
FOR row = 1 TO 24 STEP 2
  FOR col = 1 TO 70 STEP 5
    LOCATE row, col      ' Move the cursor
    PRINT firstName$
    FOR tmr = 1 TO 500    ' Timing loop
    NEXT tmr
    LOCATE row, col
    PRINT STRING$(LEN(firstName$), " ");
  NEXT col
  BEEP     ' Beep the speaker at the end of each row
NEXT row
END
```

If you want to type this program and run it, feel free to. Doing so will be good practice. However, be sure to type the program *exactly* as you see it. Although QBasic is gentle to new programmers, it can be grumpy at times, especially with typing errors.

QBasic programs are *free-form*. That is, you are free to insert extra lines and spaces just about anywhere you want. The indention of the middle lines of code is not needed, but after you learn more about QBasic, you'll see why this indention helps the readability of the program.

If you want to enter this program and run it, you can run the program in one of two ways: by selecting **Run Start** from the menu or by pressing **Shift+F5**, which is the shortcut key for **Run Start**. This is how you run any QBasic program, from the shortest to the longest.

When a program finishes, QBasic does not hurry back to the editing screen. Instead, QBasic displays the following message at the bottom of the screen:

Press any key to continue

When you press a key, the QBasic editing window returns. The message gives you a chance to look at the last part of whatever program you just ran. If QBasic raced back to the editing window when it was through, you would miss what was on-screen at the end of the program's execution.

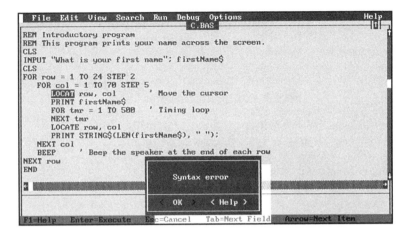

Oops! An error needs attention.

After you type the program and run it, save it to your disk. After reading a few chapters in this book, you might want to reload this program and study it to see how it works.

Looking at a Longer Program

Microsoft supplies several programs with QBasic. A couple of them, GORILLA.BAS and NIBBLES.BAS, are games you can play. As a matter of fact, this might be a good time to load and take a look at a lengthy QBasic program. To load the GORILLA.BAS program, follow these steps:

If you get an error message, such as the one shown in the figure, you typed something incorrectly. Press **OK** at the error message prompt and correct the problem. If you select **Help** at the error message, QBasic displays some advice on why you got the error. Most of the time, you probably misspelled a name somewhere.

1. Select **File** **O**pen from the menu bar.

2. At the File Name prompt, type **C:\DOS\GORILLA.BAS** and then press **Enter**. After a brief pause, you'll see this message at the top of the editing window:

    Q B a s i c   G o r i l l a s

QBasic tries to help you all it can. When QBasic encounters an error, it tries to place the text cursor on the line where the error probably happened.

If you want to quit in the middle of a QBasic program's execution, press **Ctrl+Break**. When QBasic senses a Ctrl+Break keystroke, control is given back to you in the editing window.

3. Press **Shift+F5** to run the program. (Remember that Shift+F5 is the shortcut key for **Run Start**.)

4. Don't monkey around too much! You've got a programming language to learn!

When you're back at the editing window, you can always peek back at the program's output by pressing **F4**, the shortcut key for **View Output Screen**.

Scanning a Long Program

The GORILLA.BAS program is a long one. In fact, it gives you a good chance to search through a program that takes more than a single screen. When a program is longer than one screen, your computer's screen acts like a camera that scans up and down a viewing area. Because you can view only 20 or so lines at a time, you can use the arrow keys, PageUp, and PageDown to move your computer screen through the long program.

The *scroll bar* on the right side of the screen is handy for mouse users as well. You can scroll through a long program by clicking on the scroll bar, or moving the scroll bar's *elevator box* up and down by dragging it with a mouse.

If you get a **File not found** error message, either someone deleted the GORILLA.BAS file or DOS is not installed on the C: drive in the directory named DOS. You might have to get help in finding the file if you are unfamiliar with DOS commands and directories.

The GORILLA.BAS game is a graphics-oriented game. If you have a monochrome text adapter and monitor, you'll get this error message when you attempt to run the program:

> **Sorry, you must have CGA, EGA color, or VGA graphics to play _GORILLA.BAS**

Printing a Program Listing

Often, you'll want to print a program's listing to paper. Doing so gives you an easier way to view more of the program at once. During debugging sessions of long programs, sometimes the screen size just won't give you enough room to find a problem in the code.

To print a program, follow the steps given next. (If you have the GORILLA.BAS program still loaded, it takes about 20 pages to print. You might want to load a shorter program, such as the one from the beginning of this chapter, to save paper.)

1. Turn on your printer and make sure it has paper.

2. Select File Print from the menu bar. QBasic displays a box in the middle of the screen.

3. Most of the time, you'll want the entire program to print, so press **Enter**. This selects Entire Program from the box on the screen (the *default* selection). If you wanted to print only part of a program, you could move the dot up or down to the other two options with the arrow keys or the mouse.

The Least You Need to Know

- ☞ Type the program listed in this chapter and run it for practice.

- ☞ Use the scroll bars, **arrow** keys, and **PageUp** and **PageDown** keys to move through a long program.

- ☞ Press **Ctrl+Break** when you want to quit a program before its natural conclusion.

- ☞ Don't worry about any individual program statements at this point. The next chapter begins exploring QBasic programming statements in detail.

- ☞ Don't try the two QBasic games if you don't have a graphics card and monitor. GORILLA.BAS and NIBBLES.BAS are designed for PCs with graphics adapters.

Special bonus: virtual text page.
(There's virtually nothing on it.)

Chapter 4

How Do I Explain My Program? With Remarks

In This Chapter

- ☛ REMarkable documentation
- ☛ Adding remarks

You write programs for computers, but people also read your programs. Companies that hire programmers understand the need for *readable* programs—readable not just for computers but also for people. Companies' needs change and so do the programs that companies use. Throughout this book, you will learn ways to improve the readability of your code so that you can be in demand as a programmer who writes readable code.

It has been said that a program is written once but read a thousand times. Although such a statement seems better suited in a book of proverbs, it has a lot of truth in the world of computers. The code you write must be clear so that you can easily change it in the future if the need arises. More important for the company you program for, your programs must be readable so that whoever is assigned to change your program later will be able to.

This chapter teaches you the most important part of writing readable programs. It is here that you'll learn how to add *remarks* to the programs you write.

REMarkable Documentation

Remarks are messages that explain what is happening in the program. Remarks are not for the computer; remarks are for people. Your remarks are completely ignored by QBasic, and yet they are some of the most important QBasic statements you will learn.

If you write a program that manages an inventory system, the remarks will explain how the inventory-total calculations work, how the data must be formatted for input into files, and how the inventory listings get printed.

Good habits are best learned early. Add remarks *as* you write your programs. Get in the habit now, because programmers rarely go back and add remarks after the code is written.

What if you don't program for a living, but write programs on your own for fun and profit? You don't really need remarks, right? Well, not exactly. You never know when you might have to change a program you wrote. Instead of filtering through a lot of QBasic code, you can more easily scan through remarks looking for the section that needs changing.

Consider the following QBasic statement:

IF LEFT\$(UCASE\$(C\$), 1) = "Y" THEN

This statement takes a little study, even for veteran QBasic programmers. An added short remark, however, explains the statement nicely:

IF LEFT\$(UCASE\$(C\$), 1) = "Y" THEN ' See if the user typed a Y

The next few sections describe how to add remarks, but even without explanation you can probably figure out that the text to the right of the apostrophe, ', is a remark. You can add as many blank spaces after a line of code and before the apostrophe as you want in order to make the statement and remark readable.

Because remarks are for people and not computers, don't add remarks just for the sake of adding them. Your remarks should explain to people what is going on. Consider this statement:

LET al = 21   ' Make al equal to 21

This remark is redundant (which is fancy lingo for *really stupid and unneeded*). The remark explains nothing about the statement. The remark is little more than a rewrite of the QBasic code next to it. Consider this change:

LET al = 21   **' Save the age limit for future comparisons**

Ah, now *that's* a remark! The remark truly explains what is being done by the code on the left. Remember that remarks are for people (including you) looking at your programs, not for computers. The computer doesn't need remarks! The computer understands QBasic without them.

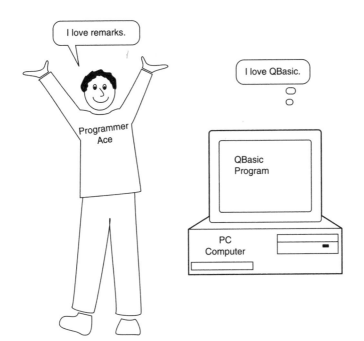

Friends don't let friends write programs without remarks.

Adding Remarks

Remarks can be specified in one of two ways: either by the **REM** statement or by a single apostrophe, ', as you saw earlier. Here is a section of code with **REM** statements:

Don't overdo remarks. Not every QBasic statement needs a remark. Add remarks only if they clarify what the code is doing. The following statement probably needs no remark:

PRINT "Hello"

Whether you know QBasic or not, you can tell that the statement prints the word Hello on-screen. A remark telling you that would add nothing.

There might be times in this book when a statement is over-remarked. You are just learning to program, and an extra remark here and there rarely hurts because you are just getting familiar with the QBasic commands.

REM The next few lines will calculate gross pay
REM then calculate the taxes so that net pay
REM then can be found.
GP = rate * hours
Taxes = GP * .35
NP = GP - Taxes

When you specify a remark with **REM**, everything following **REM** on that line is a remark, and QBasic knows to completely ignore the line. Anything can follow **REM** because people, not the computer, read the remarks. You don't have to worry about exact placement of anything after **REM**. Just be sure the remark makes sense and describes the code well.

The apostrophe remarks have the advantage of being able to reside on lines by themselves in addition to being able to follow QBasic statements on the same line. Here is a rewritten version of the section of code using both **REM** and the apostrophes:

REM The next few lines calculate payroll figures
GP = rate * hours   ' Gross pay calculation
Taxes = GP * .35   ' Compute taxes
NP = GP - Taxes   ' Net pay results

The slot machine game in Chapter 29 contains lots of remarks. Look through the program and read its remarks. Even though you know no QBasic so far, you can get an idea of how the program works just from reading the remarks.

Don't worry about which remark is the best. There is no best. The apostrophe is used more because of its flexibility, but use whichever you feel most comfortable with.

If you write programs for a living, you should know that many companies require that their programmers place their own names at the top of programs, inside remarks, including the date the programmer wrote the program. If the program later needs to be changed, the original programmer can be found to answer questions or help with the changes. Often, programmers put the program's filename in a remark at the top of the program as well.

Always end your QBasic programs with an **END** statement. **END** marks the end of the program listing and its execution. QBasic doesn't require END, but an **END** statement indicates to anyone looking at your program exactly where the end is.

Here is a complete QBasic program that includes lots of remarks for your perusal:

```
REM Filename: PAYAVG.BAS
REM Written by Pauline Programmer on July 4, 1995
REM
' This program asks users for their previous three salary
' figures, then averages the salaries.
INPUT "What was your salary three years ago"; sal1
INPUT "What was your salary two years ago"; sal2
INPUT "What was your salary last year"; sal3
avg = (sal1 + sal2 + sal3) / 3   ' Computes the average
PRINT
PRINT "The average for the three years is"; avg
END
```

Code Example

Here are two lines without remarks:

```
FOR i = 1 TO 100 STEP 5
f$ = LEFT$(full$, fNum)
```

And here are the same two statements with remarks:

```
FOR i = 1 TO 100 STEP 5    ' Count by 5s from 1 to 100
REM The next statement assigns a person's first name to
REM the variable f$.
f$ = LEFT$(full$, fNum)
```

Code Analysis

You can see how the remarks help document what is going on with the QBasic statements. A nonprogrammer ought to be able to look at your remarks and have a good idea of what is going on with the code.

The Least You Need to Know

☞ The goal of this chapter is to teach you the importance of commenting upon your code with remarks. Remarks are for people looking at your program, not for QBasic. There are two ways to begin a comment: with **REM** or with the apostrophe, '.

☞ QBasic ignores everything that follows a remark. Therefore, you would never want to put QBasic commands to the right of a remark. Many programmers put their own names in a remark statement at the top of the program to document the program's author in case there are questions later.

☞ Use remarks abundantly throughout all your programs. When in doubt, add a remark.

☞ QBasic remarks begin with **REM** or '. Use the ' for more flexibility.

☞ Don't overdo remarks. Redundant remarks are no more useful than no remarks.

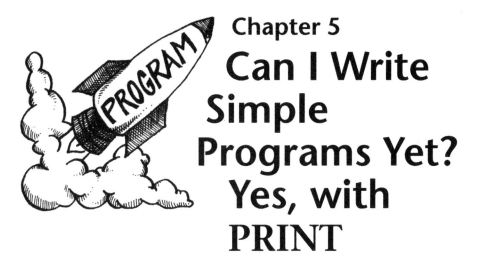

Chapter 5

Can I Write Simple Programs Yet? Yes, with PRINT

In This Chapter

- Using **PRINT** and **LPRINT**
- Starting with a clean slate
- Printing numbers
- Printing numbers and strings

The command perhaps used most in QBasic programs is **PRINT**. The **PRINT** command produces output on your screen. When you sit down to use a computer, don't you read the screen a lot? The programs you run must constantly output stuff to the screen so that the user will know what is happening. If a payroll program computed payroll figures but never printed them, the program wouldn't be worth a lot to anybody.

This chapter explains how to write simple programs that produce output. The output is sent not only to the screen but, using the **PRINT** command's cousin, the **LPRINT** command, to the printer as well.

You'll use **PRINT** for virtually anything that appears on the computer's screen. There are other ways to produce screen output, but using **PRINT** is the most common.

Using PRINT and LPRINT

PRINT has lots of formats. Even veteran QBasic programmers don't always know every format of **PRINT**, but that's OK. You need to know only a little about **PRINT** to make it handle most of your output needs. As stated in the introduction, **PRINT** sends stuff (letters, words, numbers, sentences, whatever) to the screen. **PRINT** is known as an *output* statement because it takes the output that your program produces and displays that output for the user of the program to see. Figure 5.1 explains what **PRINT** (and its cousin **LPRINT**) is all about.

The easiest thing to print is a *string.* A QBasic string is nothing more than zero or more characters enclosed in quotation marks. Both of these are strings:

"QBasic is fun!"
"448-65-0900"

Notice that strings can contain numbers as well as characters. If you have to work with a group of digits, such as a phone number, Social Security number, or ZIP code, and you are *not* going to do math with the number, keep it as a string. Later in this chapter, you'll see how to specify numbers that aren't strings.

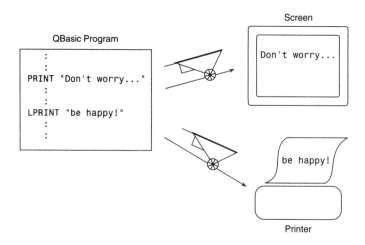

PRINT and LPRINT produce output from QBasic programs.

TECHNO NERD TEACHES...

You can indicate an empty string, called a *null string*, by placing two quotation marks next to each other like this: "". Sometimes the null string comes in handy for initializing strings that you don't yet have data for.

Here is the format for printing strings:

PRINT *string*

For example, when your QBasic program encounters the line

PRINT "QBasic is easy!"

the words **QBasic is easy!** appear on-screen. Type the following short program into QBasic and select **Run Start** to see the results. (If there is already a program in your QBasic editor, save it if you want to keep it, or select File New to erase it before entering this program.)

OOPS!

Throughout this book, when you see a new use for a command, you'll first be given the command's format. Anything in italic means that something else goes there, in this case the string of your choice. Words that aren't in italic, like **PRINT**, are required.

```
REM Program to print some strings
PRINT "My QBasic programs are so much fun"
PRINT "I think I'd like to see them run."
PRINT "I'll type the statements one by one"
PRINT "and be so glad when I am done."
END
```

Notice that each **PRINT**'s output begins on a new line when you run the program. You'll later learn how to keep **PRINT** statements from starting new lines.

Starting with a Clean Slate

If you entered and ran the preceding program, it should have worked fine, but there is a slight problem with the output. Whatever was on the output screen before you ran the program will still be there above the output of your program. It would be nice to erase the output screen completely before your program runs so that each program produces its own output on a clear screen.

QBasic supplies the **CLS** (for *clear screen*) command to do just that. When QBasic encounters **CLS**, your output screen is erased before anything is printed. Therefore, add the following statement to the top of the program just entered, and rerun the program:

```
CLS        ' Erase the screen
```

Isn't the program's output easier to read when you clear the screen first?

There is one more item related to clearing the screen. If you use **PRINT** on a line by itself, QBasic prints a blank line. In the following short program, QBasic clears the screen, prints Hello, prints a blank line, and then prints **Good-bye**.

```
CLS
PRINT "Hello"
PRINT                  ' Blank line is printed
PRINT "Good-bye"
END
```

Printing Numbers

Printing numbers is just as easy as printing strings. As a matter of fact, some people would argue that numbers are easier because you don't have to enclose numbers in quotation marks. If you want to print the numbers from 1 to 3, here is how you can do it:

```
PRINT 1
PRINT 2
PRINT 3
```

Of course, you could have enclosed the numbers in quotation marks and QBasic would have still printed the numbers from 1 to 3 on separate lines.

Printing Numbers and Strings

Don't have your QBasic programs print numbers on the screen or printer without accompanying messages that tell what the numbers mean. For example, if you wanted to tell the user to enter three values, which is clearer? This:

3

Or this:

You must enter 3 values.

QBasic always prints a space before and after positive numbers. Therefore, the 1, 2, and 3 would print with a space before them (the space wouldn't be there if you enclosed the numbers in quotation marks). QBasic prints a negative sign (and no space) before negative numbers.

Obviously, describing your numeric output is best.

Any time you want to print more than one value on a single line, whether those values are strings, numbers, or a combination of both, separate each item with a semicolon, ;. For example, you can print the preceding line like this:

PRINT "You must enter"; 3; "values."

Of course, you could have enclosed the entire line in quotation marks and you wouldn't have to use the semicolon. However, you need to understand the separating semicolon so that you'll understand how to output the data described in the next chapter.

Code Example

```
REM The following output statements can go to the printer
REM if you add an L to each of the PRINT statements.
PRINT "This is the first line printed in the program."
```

```
PRINT              ' Prints a blank line
PRINT "I'll now print some numbers:"
PRINT 10
PRINT 20
PRINT 30
PRINT "That's a big"; 10; "-"; 4
END
```

If you put a trailing semicolon at the end of a **PRINT** statement, a subsequent **PRINT** output will not appear on the next line. The following two **PRINT** statements print both words on one line because of the first **PRINT**'s trailing semicolon:

> PRINT "Miami, ";
> PRINT "Florida"

Code Analysis

The program prints a string, a blank line, another string, then three numbers on-screen. Each of these output values appears on a different line of output.

The last line of output prints two strings with two embedded numbers between them. The semicolon outputs values on the same line next to each other. The last line produces this output:

That's a big 10 - 4

The space appears on either side of the dash because QBasic always leaves a space before and after positive numbers.

The Least You Need to Know

☞ The goal of this chapter is to teach you how to send output to your screen or printer from your QBasic program. The **PRINT** command sends output to the screen, and the **LPRINT** command sends output to the printer.

☞ **PRINT** is one of the most common QBasic commands and is used in almost every program. After all, most programs write to the screen. You can print text by enclosing it in quotation marks and print numbers by listing them to the right of **PRINT** and **LPRINT**.

☛ Use the **PRINT** statement to send output to the screen.

☛ Use the **LPRINT** statement to send output to the printer.

☛ Use the **CLS** command to erase the screen.

☛ Don't forget to enclose all string data in quotation marks.

☛ Don't print numbers without some kind of descriptive string.

No, this is not a printing error.
The page truly is blank.

Chapter 6

How Do I Store Stuff? Using Variables!

In This Chapter

- ☞ Variables everywhere
- ☞ Naming variables
- ☞ Putting stuff in variables
- ☞ Printing values in variables

QBasic must have a way to store numbers and strings. If you have ever worked with a calculator that had a memory, you know that the memory enables you to store values so that you can retrieve them later. It is much easier to use the memory than to find a pencil and write down the result that you'll need later. The memory also keeps you from having to calculate the same formula more than once.

QBasic uses *variables* to store data. A variable is a place in memory that you attach a name to in your program. When you store something in a variable, you can later retrieve the value by using the variable name.

The word **data** is actually plural for *datum*. Who uses *datum* anymore? We'll stick to the more commonly used *data* for both single and multiple values.

Variables Everywhere

A QBasic program might use many variables. The number of variables you need depends on the application you are programming. If you have lots of different values to track, such as if you're performing a scientific experiment that requires hundreds of calculations, you might need hundreds of variables to hold the results. If you are writing a simple averaging program or writing a program to keep track of a phone list in a disk file, you might not need many variables.

There is no practical limit as to how many variables you can have in a single program. QBasic enables you to have as many as you need. When you need a new variable, you just refer to it by a different name. Therefore, this chapter will explain how to name variables (because you are responsible for that), how to store data in variables, and how to use variables in your programs.

Think of variables as acting like boxes inside your computer. The variables to your computer are a lot like post office boxes inside a post office. Each post office box has a unique number; each variable has a unique name. No two variables can have the same name.

If two or more variables could have the same name, how would QBasic know which one you wanted to use when you used the name?

There are many types of QBasic variables, and this book will explain each one as we go along. However, these are the two primary kinds of variables:

☞ Numeric

☞ String

Variables hold data that can change. In the previous program, you saw how to print *constant* data. When you see

PRINT 25

you know that a **25** prints no matter how many times you run the program. The **25** is known as a *constant* because it remains constant. Variables hold data, such as salary figures, ages, amounts, totals, and other values that can change during a program's execution.

This is easy: *numeric variables* hold numbers, and *string variables* hold strings.

Naming Variables

Learn how to name variables, because *you* are responsible for the names. That is, when you need a variable, you have to assign a unique name to the variable. QBasic variable names can range from 1 to 40 characters, and they must begin with a letter of the alphabet. After the letter, a variable can contain numbers or letters. All the following examples are valid variable names:

sales94   Amount   AGE   qtr4Pay93   i

It does not matter whether you use uppercase or lowercase letters. You must, however, be consistent. If you first call a variable **Amount**, don't call it **aMOUNT** later, or QBasic will think you renamed the variable and will change the first one you entered to the most recent case.

Give your variables meaningful names. If you want to store your friend's age, **friendAge** is a much better name than **x12ERddss**, even though QBasic doesn't care which you use.

Everything just said about variable names holds for *numeric variables only*. If you want to store a string in a variable, the string variable name must end in a dollar sign, **$**. Therefore, **partNo** can hold numbers, but **partNo$** can be assigned only strings (either string constants enclosed in quotation marks or other string variables).

Putting Stuff in Variables

Before you put anything into a variable, QBasic puts a zero in the variable for you. You can put something else in the variable with an *assignment* statement. Here is the format of the assignment statement:

Don't give a variable the same name as a QBasic command. For instance, QBasic will not enable you to name a variable **END** or **CLS**.

[LET] *variableName = expression*

Don't actually type the square brackets. When you see square brackets in command formats, the brackets indicate optional keywords. You don't have to type **LET** when you put values into variables.

Here is how you would store a different number in two variables named **Amt1** and **Amt2**:

```
Amt1 = 2932      ' Stores 2932 into Amt1
Amt2 = 9485      ' Stores 9485 into Amt2
```

You can use the four simple math operators seen in Table 6.1 to store results of calculations in variables.

Table 6.1   The four QBasic math operators

Operator	Description
+	Addition
–	Subtraction
*	Multiplication
/	Division

The following statement puts a 15 in the variable named age:

```
age = 10 + 5
```

The **LET** is optional, so many programmers don't type it. The following assignment is exactly the same as the previous statement:

```
LET age = 10 + 5
```

A calculation can even contain other variables. Consider the following example:

```
sales = 39456.54
costOfSales = 10233.90
netSales = sales - costOfSales
```

The variable named **netSales** contains the difference between the total sales and the cost of sales. (See how meaningful variable names make the code clearer?)

Here's some code that stores two names in two string variables:

> **company1$ = "Kranco, Inc."**
> **company2$ = "Super Amalgamated"**

You know that **company1$** and **company2$** can hold only strings because their names end with a dollar sign.

Study the figure to see how these assignment statements store data in memory:

> **age = 46**
> **myName$ = "Terrie"**
> **total = 6 + 7**

```
                                Variable
                                Name          Memory

          age = 46              age             :
                                                46
       myName$ = "Terrie"       myName$         :
                                                Terrie
          total = 6 + 7         total           :
                                                13
                                                :
```

All variables have names and values. The assignment statement stores values in variables.

Printing Values in Variables

QBasic makes it easy to print values stored in variables. Just follow a **PRINT** with the variable name. **PRINT** will not print the variable names themselves. To show you how **PRINT** operates, the following **PRINT** statements produce the output shown after them.

```
a = 10 * 20
b = 6.8 / 2
n$ = "Tony"
PRINT a
PRINT "The value of b is"; b
PRINT n$
PRINT "The value of n$ is "; n$
```

```
200
The value of b is 3.4
Tony
The value of n$ is Tony
```

Code Example

```
REM This program stores and computes several variables
REM before printing them to the screen.
i = 8
j = 10
k = 20
n = i + j + k
x = i * j * k
word$ = "QBasic"
PRINT "The value of i + j + k is"; n
PRINT "The value of i * j * k is"; x
PRINT "The value of word$ is "; word$
END
```

Code Analysis

The program first assigns three numbers to three numeric variables, **i**, **j**, and **k**. A fourth variable, **n**, holds the sum of the three variables, and a fifth variable, **x**, holds the product of the three variables.

A string variable is then assigned the string **QBasic**. A dollar sign has to follow all string variable names. A variable name without a dollar sign is a numeric variable (until you learn how to use more advanced variable-definition commands, discussed in Part V of this book).

If you print a variable using its name, as done in the last three **PRINT** statements, the value of the variable, not the variable name, goes to the screen.

The Least You Need to Know

☞ The goal of this chapter is to show you how data is stored in QBasic programs. You don't always know every value needed in a program at the time you write a program. Often, you need to store values and later change them (just as you might do in a more limited fashion on a calculator with several memory storage buttons).

☞ Variables are the holders of a program's data. You store data in a variable by using the equal sign, =. Variables can hold numbers and string data. Before you can use a variable, you must think up a name for the variable that matches the variable naming rules. If you like, you can use the QBasic math operators to calculate values to put in variables.

☞ Use variables to hold data that can change.

☞ Learn the variable naming rules so that you can assign meaningful names to the variables you use.

☞ Print variables by specifying their names after **PRINT**.

☞ Use the math operators to assign calculated results to variables.

☞ Don't give two different variables the same name.

☞ Don't use a command name for the name of a variable.

Here's that blank page thing again.

Chapter 7

Can I Ask the User Questions? Yes, with INPUT

In This Chapter

- Looking at **INPUT**
- Mixing the prompt with **INPUT**
- Another **INPUT** option

This chapter picks up where the preceding one left off. Chapter 6 showed you how to produce output on the screen and printer. This chapter shows you how to get data from the keyboard (called *input*). A program must be able to receive input from the user sitting at the keyboard. Suppose you were writing a program that calculated daily sales totals for a candy store. At the time you write the program, you have no idea how much candy will be sold. Instead, the program will have to find out each day exactly how much was sold.

The **INPUT** command accepts keyboard data. When you get to a place in a program that requires keyboard entry, use the **INPUT** command. There are several formats of **INPUT**, and this chapter explains the most common ones.

Looking at INPUT

The **INPUT** command does the opposite job of **PRINT**. As the figure shows, **INPUT** receives data from the keyboard and stores that data in variables. Before getting data with **INPUT**, your program should tell the user exactly what kind of data value is expected.

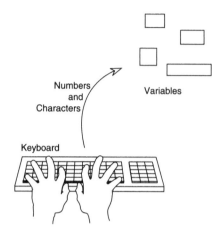

INPUT stores what the user enters into variables.

INPUT has several formats. Here is the easiest:

INPUT *variableName*

INPUT gets numbers, characters, or strings into variables.

The *variableName* can be any valid QBasic variable. Both of the following examples are valid **INPUT** commands. The first one inputs a number from the keyboard, and the second one inputs a string.

INPUT amt
INPUT lastName$

When QBasic encounters **INPUT**, a question mark (**?**) appears on the screen, and the program waits for the user to enter a value. **INPUT** knows when the user is done because the user has to press **Enter** after typing the input value.

Programmers often print a *prompt* before an **INPUT**. A prompt is just a message that explains what the **INPUT** is looking for. For example, if you wanted the user to enter his or her age, your program might contain these two statements:

> PRINT "What is your age"
> INPUT age

Because **INPUT** always produces a question mark, you do not need to put a question mark inside the prompt. However, in the preceding pair of statements, the question mark appears on the line following the prompt, like this:

> **What is your age**
> **?**

You learned in the preceding chapter how to fix this problem. Remember how the trailing semicolon works? A trailing semicolon keeps the cursor from moving down to the next line after a **PRINT**. Here is a better way to ask for the age:

> PRINT "What is your age";
> ' Suppress the cursor movement
> INPUT age

The following program asks the user for the preceding three days' temperature readings. The average for those three temperatures is computed and printed.

When the computer gets to this **PRINT**, the user sees this:

What is your age?

When the user types a number, followed by the **Enter** keystroke, that number is stored in the age variable, and the program then continues.

```
' Program that produces a running average of
' the previous 3-day temperature readings.
CLS
PRINT "What is the first day's temperature";
INPUT day1
PRINT "What is the second day's temperature";
INPUT day2
PRINT "What is the third day's temperature";
```

If the user runs the program several times, entering different values, the program prints a different answer each time. Therefore, with **INPUT**, you now have programs that respond to changing conditions without requiring rewriting of the code itself.

```
INPUT day3
' Calculate and print the average
avg = (day1 + day2 + day3) / 3
PRINT            ' Prints a blank line
PRINT "The average temperature was"; avg
END
```

Here is a sample run from this program:

What is the first day's temperature? 87.5
What is the second day's temperature? 92.6
What is the third day's temperature? 90.1

The average temperature was 90.06667

In the preceding example, the average value printed with five decimal places. In Chapter 8, "How Do I Spruce Up My Output?" you'll see how to limit the number of decimal places printed.

Mixing the Prompt with INPUT

QBasic enables you to combine the prompt directly inside the **INPUT** statement itself. Therefore, instead of using the **PRINT-INPUT** combination every time you need to get input, you need only use **INPUT**. Here is the format of the expanded **INPUT**:

> INPUT *"Prompt message"; variableName*

An example is worth a thousand words of description. Both of the following sets of code are the same:

> **PRINT "What is your name";**
> **INPUT name$**

and

> **INPUT "What is your name"; name$**

When your computer reaches the **INPUT**, the user sees this:

> **What is your name?**

The value the user then types will go into the name$ variable.

Another INPUT Option

There is one more thing you should know about **INPUT**. If you follow the **INPUT** prompt with a comma rather than a semicolon, QBasic does not print a question mark. There could be times when you want to prompt the user with something other than a question. For instance, the following **INPUT** does not automatically display a question mark:

> **INPUT "Please type your answer and press Enter when done...", ans**

Why would you ever want to type two lines when a single one will do the same thing? You wouldn't.

When QBasic gets to this **INPUT**, the user sees this:

> **Please type your answer and press Enter when done...**

Code Example

```
REM A program that demonstrates several versions of INPUT
PRINT "What is your name";
INPUT nam$
INPUT "What is your age"; age
INPUT iq
INPUT "Hurry, type the result of 5 * 9: ", ans
PRINT
PRINT "Your name is "; nam$
PRINT "You are"; age; "years old."
PRINT "Your IQ is"; iq
PRINT "You said that 5 * 9 is"; ans
END
```

Code Analysis

The program demonstrates the different methods, some good and some not as good, that you can use to get input from the user sitting at the keyboard.

The first two occurrences of **INPUT** in Chapter 29's slot-machine game suppress the question mark.

The first **INPUT** is preceded by a **PRINT** that asks the user a question. The second **INPUT** statement shows how to eliminate the **PRINT** statement. **INPUT** is capable of displaying a prompt without a separate **PRINT** statement.

Before computer keyboards and video screens, all input had to be entered through punched cards and ticker-tape devices! (This was back in ancient times when archaic writing tools called typewriters were still in use.)

The third **INPUT** is the most poorly designed one in the program. The user is supposed to type his or her IQ, but the user has no idea what is being asked for. Without a prompting message, the user could type anything, regardless of his or her IQ.

The final **INPUT** suppresses the **INPUT** statement's question mark by preceding the input variable with a comma.

The values input by the user are then printed with appropriate descriptions before them.

The Least You Need to Know

- ☞ The goal of this chapter is to teach you how to get input from the user sitting at the keyboard. The user is anyone (including you) who runs the programs that you or somebody else writes.

- ☞ Use **INPUT** to accept keyboard input into variables. **INPUT** displays a question mark unless you suppress the question mark by putting a comma before the INPUT variable name.

- ☞ Always prompt the user by printing a message indicating what kind of input you want from the user. If a question mark appears out of the blue when a user runs your program, the user has no idea what you are asking for if you don't print a prompt first.

- ☞ Use **INPUT** to request values from the user.

- ☞ Remember that **INPUT** always displays a question mark unless you suppress the question mark by using a comma after the prompt.

- ☞ Don't ask for a value unless you prompt the user first. The prompt lets the user know exactly what is expected.

Chapter 8

How Do I Spruce Up My Output? With PRINT Formatting

In This Chapter

- ☞ Add flair with color
- ☞ Line up: printing in columns
- ☞ Moving the cursor around the screen
- ☞ Beep-beep!
- ☞ Print formatting

There is much more you can do with **PRINT** and **LPRINT**. For starters, if you have a color monitor, you might want to output color text rather than drab black on white. After you add color, you can improve your output even more by printing data in columns and formatting your numbers so that they look exactly the way you want them to look.

Anything you can do to improve the look of your program's output helps put the user at ease. Nobody likes to see dollar and cent values printed to four decimal places. Also, anybody sitting in front of a computer using your program all day will appreciate reading color screens. Adding a beep before printing an error message will really wake your user, especially if you print the error in color! This chapter explains how to do both.

In this book, the white page is the background and the black ink is the foreground.

Add Flair with Color

If you are writing programs for someone with a color monitor and color graphics adapter (a large percentage of computer users today have both), you can add pizzazz to your programs by coloring the output. The **COLOR** command enables you to determine exactly what colors your output will appear in. Here is the format of **COLOR**:

COLOR [foreground#] [, background#]

After you specify colors with a **COLOR** statement, all subsequent **PRINT**s will produce text in that color. Any output that was printed before the **COLOR** statement remains unchanged.

The tear-out card in this book lists all of QBasic's colors and the numbers that go with the colors. To specify a color, you must use its number in the **COLOR** statement. The foreground color is the color of the text, and the background color is the color of the background screen.

As the format suggests, both the foreground and the background colors are optional—you have to specify only one of them. If you specify only a foreground color number, the background is left unchanged. If you specify only a background color number (the comma indicates that the value is background and not foreground), the foreground remains unchanged.

To print the message This is colorful in white text on a blue background, you can use these lines:

```
COLOR 15, 1  ' Bright white on a blue background
PRINT "This is colorful"
```

As you can see, **COLOR** affects only *future* printing. If you want the entire screen to become the color you request, follow **COLOR** with a **CLS**, like this:

```
COLOR 10, 7  ' Green letters on a white background
CLS          ' Clear the entire screen and give it a
             ' white background
PRINT "This is green on white"
```

If you wanted to print bright yellow lettering on the blue background just generated, you could use these lines:

COLOR 14   ' Bright yellow foreground
PRINT "This is yellow text still on blue"

To change the background to red, you could use these lines:

COLOR , 4   ' Notice the comma
PRINT "Yellow on red"

Don't overdo colors! Too many colors make your screens look "busy," and your user will more easily tire of the program.

If you add 16 to the foreground color, QBasic causes your output to blink on and off. Warning messages such as **Be sure the printer has paper!** might get more attention if you print them in blinking letters.

Line Up: Printing in Columns

If you want output to appear in a specific column, use the **TAB()** function. **TAB()** is called a *function* and not a *command,* but the difference at this point is minor. Use **TAB()** with **PRINT** and **LPRINT**. If you want to print tables of output, you might want to stick tabs between your printed output to force the output to appear in certain columns.

Back in prehistoric times, people used typewriters. As you probably know, with typewriters you can set tab stops. QBasic's **TAB()** function works like the typewriter's tab stop.

Here is the format of **TAB()**:

TAB(*value*)

You generally bury **TAB( )** inside a **PRINT** or an **LPRINT**. Here is where an example will help a lot. Suppose you wanted to print the word Tampa in column 20 and the word Florida in column 32. Why you would want to do that is beyond me! Anyway, this statement does the printing:

> PRINT TAB(20); "Tampa"; TAB(32); "Florida"

Use **LOCATE** to move the cursor all around the screen. You can even print "up" the screen by locating the cursor on a lower row and printing, then locating and printing on each row above the preceding one.

Moving the Cursor Around the Screen

The **LOCATE** command moves the cursor to whatever row and column you want it to appear in. Suppose you want to print a title on the second line of the screen starting in the 20th column. You can use **LOCATE** to move the cursor, and then a **PRINT** will begin printing there. Here is the format of **LOCATE**:

> LOCATE [row#] [, column#]

The **row#** must be a number from 1 to 25 (because there are 25 screen rows), and the **column#** must be from 1 to 80 (because, you guessed it, there are 80 columns). If you specify only the **row#** or the **column#**, then only that position is changed from the cursor's current placement. Here is the pair of statements that prints a message on row 5, column 36:

> LOCATE 5, 36
> PRINT "Get located!"

LOCATE enables you to overwrite parts of the screen you have already written to.

Beep-Beep!

Although you might not consider a bell ringing to be output, it is. When you want to get the user's attention, you can signal the user by buzzing the computer's bell with the **BEEP** command. Here is the format of **BEEP**:

> BEEP

What could be easier? Every time QBasic comes across **BEEP** in your program, the computer's bell rings.

Adding a **BEEP** and blinking a message flashing in red letters will *really* get your user's attention if you need to!

Print Formatting

There are two commands that correspond to **PRINT** and **LPRINT** called **PRINT USING** and **LPRINT USING**. There is a lot to the USING keyword, but most of the time you will need **USING** just to format numbers so that they print with a certain number of decimal places. Before looking at an example, take a look at the format of the **PRINT USING** command:

The **LPRINT USING** command format looks just like that of **PRINT USING**.

PRINT USING *"formatString"; data*

The *formatString* is a string that contains the *look* that the **data** is to take. Often, you will see a *control code* inside the *formatString*. The control code is usually one of the following: #, ., ,, or &. When numbers are being printed, the # indicates a new digit in the number. For example, to print the number **456.7223** to one decimal place, you can use this:

Of course, if you wanted the number printed to one decimal place, you could have just printed **456.7**. The power of formatting shows itself when you print variables that contain data which needs formatting.

PRINT USING "###.#"; 456.7223   ' Prints 456.7

If the number is smaller than the format string, QBasic pads with blanks. For example, the PRINT USING statement

PRINT USING "######.## ######.## ######.##"; 5, 6, 7

prints this:

5.00   6.00   7.00

The format strings round for you. Here is what you get if you print **456.7923** with the preceding format string:

456.8

If the number is larger than the format string you specify, QBasic prints the entire number with a percent sign, %, before it to get your attention that something is incorrect with the format string.

To print strings combined with numbers, you can use the & inside a format string to indicate the placement of the string. Study the following example **PRINT USING** statements to see how QBasic treats different versions of format strings.

```
' Short example to demonstrate USING format strings
num1 = 12345.67
st1$ = "Frank makes"
st2$ = "dollars a year"
PRINT USING "#####.#"; num1
PRINT USING "& #####.## &"; st1$; num1; st2$
PRINT USING "Frank makes $#####,.## dollars a year"; num1
END
```

Here is the output from these **PRINT USING** statements:

```
12345.7
Frank makes 12345.67 dollars a year
Frank makes $12,345.67 dollars a year
```

The figure helps explain the second **PRINT USING** statement. Remember that the format string simply describes how the subsequent data will look.

The format string describes the look of the data being printed.

PRINT USING is not exactly the easiest thing in the world to get familiar with. As mentioned earlier, you will most often use the ####.## code (with more or fewer pound signs depending on your needs) to print dollars and cents. Non-money values and strings typically print well without a **USING** format string.

Notice that if you precede the decimal point inside a format string with a comma, QBasic inserts commas where needed in the number.

The **PRINT USING** was derived from an older programming language named FOR-TRAN. QBasic, however, improves on FORTRAN's formatted output because FORTRAN requires two statements to do what a single **PRINT USING** does.

Code Example

```
BEEP
COLOR 4, 10   ' Green on red, Blecch!
PRINT "Hey, you're in the green!"
PRINT "You've sold QBasic programs and made a fortune!"
END
```

Code Analysis

This short program first rings the PC's bell and then changes the colors of screen output to green letters on a red background. The printed messages then appear in those colors.

The Least You Need to Know

☞ The goal of this chapter is to show you ways to liven up your output by ringing the computer's bell and displaying colors on-screen. Of course, you can display colors only if your PC's hardware supports colors. Most people who own PCs have color monitors and adapter cards that can produce colorful output.

continues

continued

☞ **BEEP** is one of the easiest commands in QBasic because it requires nothing but the single-word command **BEEP** to ring the computer's bell. The **COLOR** statement uses a table of color codes to set up the screen for colorful output. **COLOR** affects only future output, not printed output that is already on-screen when the **COLOR** command executes.

☞ Use **COLOR** to make your output screens more appealing.

☞ Use **BEEP** to get your user's attention.

☞ If you want to print dollar amounts, the **PRINT USING** command will help you format your output.

☞ Don't overdo **COLOR** and **BEEP**. Too much will confuse rather than help the user.

☞ Relax! This chapter contained more details than any other so far. The rest of this book will use the material you learned here, so you'll get lots of review as you go along.

Chapter 9

How Does QBasic Do Math? With Operators

In This Chapter

- ☞ Additional operators
- ☞ Exponentiation
- ☞ Integer division with \
- ☞ The **MOD** squad
- ☞ The order of operators

QBasic uses *operators* to perform math calculations. In Chapter 6 ("How Do I Store Stuff?") you learned about four operators (the ones that add, subtract, multiply, and divide). There are more operators, and this chapter explains the additional ones. Not only must you understand the operators, but you must understand the *ordering* that QBasic uses to perform calculations using those operators.

QBasic does not always use a symbol, such as +, for its operators. The operator named **MOD** looks like a command. There is a good reason why QBasic, unlike most programming languages, does not stick to symbols for all of

OOPS!

Don't you just hate math? If you do, you're in the right field, because QBasic does your math for you if you learn how to set up the computations correctly.

its operators. I just don't know what the reason is. Anyway, that's the way it is, and knowing that, you'll have fewer questions as you read through this chapter.

Additional Operators

This table lists the QBasic operators that are available in addition to +, –, *, and /. The sections that follow explain each of these additional operators.

Table 9.1   The Additional QBasic Operators

Operator	Usage	Name and description
^	2 ^ 5	Called the *exponentiation operator*, ^ raises a number to a specified power.
\	16 \ 3	Called the *integer division operator*, \ produces an integer result.
MOD	14 MOD 3	Called the *modulus operator*, MOD calculates the remainder after integer division takes place.

Don't confuse the integer division, \, with the regular division, /. They slant in opposite directions.

Exponentiation

The term *exponentiation* sounds a lot hairier than it really is. Even *math-sensitive* persons (the politically correct term these days for people who are math lame-brains) can understand raising numbers to powers. Often you see exponentiation written using a superscript for the exponent. In other words, if you were to see a 5 raised to the third power, you would see it written like this:

$$5^3$$

That means multiply 5 by itself three times: 5 times 5 times 5 is 125. In QBasic, we could store the same value in a variable by doing this:

ans = 5 ^ 3

Quickly, what is stored in **ans** in the next statement?

ans = 2 ^ 4

Because **2 ^ 4** means to multiply 2 times itself four times, and 2 times 2 times 2 times 2 equals 16, **ans** stores the number **16**.

TECHNO NERD TEACHES...

You can take the *n*th root of a number by raising it to a fractional value. For instance, to take the fifth root of 243, you could do this:

num = 243 ^ (1/5)

You'll read a little later in this chapter why the parentheses are needed. By the way, the fifth root of 243 is 3.

Integer Division with \

An integer is any number without a decimal point. Often we say that integers are whole numbers. All of these numbers are integers:

32   912   0   -121

None of these are integers:

32.333   0.0   -123.64   912.0

In a nutshell, using the \ tells QBasic to divide and throw away the remainder. Although **9 / 2** is **4.5**, **9 \ 2** (notice that the *integer divide* sign was used) produces **4**, which is the whole number answer.

Here's a neat use for the \
operator. Suppose you were
writing a program that
calculated change. To find
out how many five-dollar
bills were in the variable
change, you could do this:

numFives = change \ 5

Sometimes we can think of remainders as being
whole numbers themselves. For instance, another
way of looking at **9 / 2** is that it is **4** with a remainder of **1**. The \ always produces the whole number
portion. The next operator, **MOD**, returns the
remainder.

The MOD Squad

As just mentioned, **MOD** performs the other half of
\. Whereas \ produces the integer portion of a
division answer, **MOD** produces the integer remain-
der. Therefore, **9 MOD 2** produces an answer of **1** because **9** divided by **2** is
4 with a remainder of **1**.

The following code reviews all the math operators:

```
PRINT "2 + 3 is"; 2 + 3
PRINT "6 - 4 is"; 6 - 4
PRINT "2 * 3 is"; 2 * 3
PRINT "12 / 7 is"; 12 / 7
PRINT "12 \ 7 is"; 12 \ 7
PRINT "12 MOD 7 is"; 12 MOD 7
PRINT "3 ^ 6 is"; 3 ^ 6
END
```

Here is the output from these **PRINT** statements:

Notice that you can print
the results of calculations
directly without having to
store them in variables first.

```
2 + 3 is 5
6 - 4 is 2
2 * 3 is 6
12 / 7 is 1.714286
12 \ 7 is 1
12 MOD 7 is 5
3 ^ 6 is 729
```

The Order of Operators

QBasic does not always calculate from left to right. There is an order to QBasic's calculations. You'll find a table on the tear-out card called the *Order of Operators* table. This table explains that addition and subtraction are always calculated last, no matter where they appear within other operators. For example, the following statement does *not* store **14** in **ans**:

Here's a good use for the immediate execution window at the bottom of the QBasic editing screen. Press **F6** (the shortcut key to move between windows) and type **PRINT 20 * 30.** When you press **Enter,** QBasic displays the answer. Press any key and you're back to the editing window. You can try statements in the immediate execution window without affecting anything in the program itself.

ans = 3 + 4 * 2

A **14** would be stored in **ans** if QBasic did the addition first, but it does not. As the Order of Operators table tells you, multiplication is higher in the table, and therefore multiplication is said to *take precedence* over addition. Because the multiplication is performed first, the **4** is multiplied by the **2** to get **8**, and *then* the **3** is added to the **8**, to result in an **11** being stored in **ans**.

The parentheses take precedence over the other operators. Therefore, if you wanted the addition calculated first, you could group the addition inside parentheses like this:

ans = (3 + 4) * 2   ' A 14 is stored in ans now

Here is a long calculation with each step shown for you. If you follow the Order of Operators, you'll understand how each step was chosen.

ans = 6 + 40 - 8 / 2 MOD 3 * 2 ^ 3
                    \ /
       6 + 40 - 8 / 2 MOD 3 * 8
              \ /
          6 + 40 - 4 MOD 3 * 8
                    \ /
          6 + 40 - 4 MOD 24
          \ /
            6 + 40 - 4
            \ /
              46 - 4
              \ /
     42   (The value stored in ans)

Code Example

```
id = 100 \ 3   ' Integer division
PRINT "100 \ 3 is"; id
PRINT 1 + 2 + 3 + 4 + 5 * 2
PRINT (1 + 2 + 3 + 4 + 5) * 2
END
```

Code Analysis

In the example, the first two statements compute and print the integer division (no fraction or remainder is kept) of **100** divided by **3** (producing a value of **33**). The next two **PRINT** statements produce very different values indeed. The first **PRINT** prints the value of **20** because the **5 * 2** results in **10** and the **1** and **2** and **3** and **4** are then added to the **10**. In the second **PRINT**, the numbers **1** through **5** are first added, and the result, **15**, is multiplied by **2** giving an answer of **30**.

The Least You Need to Know

☛ The goal of this chapter is to explore the QBasic operators and show you how they work. QBasic multiplies, adds, and subtracts in the way you would expect. There are three operators related to division: /, \, and **MOD**. The forward slash, /, divides two numbers as usual. The backslash, \, performs integer division. Integer division always produces a whole-number result and discards any remainder. The **MOD** operator picks up where \ leaves off by computing the remainder of an integer division. There is another operator, ^, which calculates exponentiation.

☛ When you combine math operators, you must always be aware of QBasic's order of operation. QBasic always performs exponentiation before multiplication and division. QBasic saves addition and subtraction for last. You can override the order by adding parentheses to force evaluation of specific operations before the evaluation would normally take place.

☛ Let QBasic calculate everything for you.

☛ Use ^, **MOD**, and \ to compute exponentiation, remainder, and integer division.

☛ Pay attention to the Order of Operators when setting up your calculations.

☛ Use parentheses. Parentheses override the rest of the operator order, and they clearly express what you want done.

☛ Don't confuse the regular division operator, /, with the integer division operator, \.

This page unintentionally left blank.

How Do I Specify Different Data? With Extended Data Types

In This Chapter

- ☛ Literals and constants
- ☛ Numeric data types
- ☛ Scientific notation

This chapter could be your least favorite in the book. It is not difficult or boring, but you might wonder why you need to know the material presented here. This chapter discusses the various *data types* in QBasic. You already know about two of them, numbers and strings. This chapter explains why there are different types of numbers and describes the various ways to specify each of the numeric data types.

As you read through the rest of the book, you'll better understand why these concepts are being taught here. When you want to work with a number that is extremely large, you might consider storing that number in a special kind of numeric variable designed to hold large numbers.

Stay with this chapter and your knowledge of it will pay dividends later. Some beginning QBasic programmers put off learning this chapter's material too long because it looks like a lot of math that they'll never need. Trust me, you'll need it again and again. QBasic does all the math for you as long as you understand how to set things up.

Most of this chapter teaches you new terms that you'll need to understand as you progress through the rest of the book.

By the time you finish this chapter, you'll understand all the different variable suffix characters that QBasic offers as well. You already know that string variable names must end in dollar signs. The different numeric variables end in different data type suffix characters as well.

Literals and Constants

When you type a number or string in a QBasic program, you are typing a *constant* or a *literal*. Both words mean the same thing. Each of these are literals and constants:

```
534
-39.7
"Sally"
"1013 N. Illinois Ave."
```

The opposite of literals and constants are *variables*. The contents of variables can change (they *vary*, and that's why they're called variables).

Numeric Data Types

You already know what an integer is. The preceding chapter explained that an integer is a whole number without a decimal point. There are actually two kinds of QBasic integers: an integer and a *long integer*. The difference between them is determined by the range of numbers each can contain. Basically, a long integer can be larger than an integer. In a moment, you'll see the range of values that can appear in both kinds of integers.

The opposite of an integer is a *real number* (a number with a decimal point). However, as with integers, QBasic enables you to use two different kinds of real numbers depending on the range of values you want to represent. A *single-precision* number is one of QBasic's real number data types, and a *double-precision* number is the other kind of real number data type.

A table will help explain everything. This one lists each of QBasic's numeric data types and the range of values that each can hold.

Table 10.1   QBasic's Numeric Data Types and Their Ranges

Data Type	Data Type Suffix	Range
Integer	%	-32768 to 32767
Long integer	&	-2147483648 to 2147483647
Single-precision	! (or none)	-3.402823×10^{38} to 3.402823×10^{38}
Double-precision	#	$-1.79769313486231 \times 10^{308}$ to $1.79769313486231 \times 10^{308}$

The funny-looking numbers in the last two entries of the table are called *scientific notation*. You'll see how to interpret scientific notation numbers a little later in this chapter.

The primary reason for learning the different kinds of numbers is that there is a different kind of variable for each of those data types. All the numeric variables you have used so far have been single-precision variables. But what if you wanted to store a huge number (such as a QBasic programmer's annual salary) in a variable? If you want to, you might have to use a larger precision variable.

After you use a variable with a suffix, you must always use the suffix. In other words, don't name a variable **sales#** in the top of a program and then **sales** at the bottom. QBasic would think they were two different variables.

Just as you use the dollar sign on string variables, you can use the data type suffixes in the table to indicate a specific type of numeric variable. Here are some lines that store different values in each type of variable:

```
a% = 123                  ' Integer
b& = 642346654            ' Long integer
c! = 532.34               ' Single-precision
d# = 39493344.233929      ' Double-precision
```

There is one last point you should understand: QBasic sometimes puts data type suffixes at the end of numeric constants, and you can do the same. QBasic does this to remind you that the number might be too large to fit within the smaller precision. For example, type the following line in QBasic:

i = 123456.78

What happened? QBasic immediately changed the statement to this:

i = 123456.78#

If double-precision variables and long integer variables hold large numbers as well as small, why not always use them? It takes longer for QBasic to calculate and print the larger variables. Therefore, for efficiency, don't use the larger-precision variable types unless you really need to hold numbers within their wide ranges.

The variable **i** is single-precision because there is no # suffix and the value is small enough to fit in a single-precision variable. However, QBasic still insists on treating the number as if it were double-precision.

If you do not specify a data type suffix, QBasic assumes that the variable is single-precision. Therefore, these variables are identical and indicate the only data type suffix that is optional:

myVal

and

myVal!

Scientific Notation

Don't let the name throw you! Scientific notation is easy to understand. Even if you don't ever plan to use scientific notation, QBasic sometimes displays results in scientific notation, so you should understand how to interpret it. (You also need to know what the last two lines in the previous table mean!)

Scientific notation is a shortcut method for specifying extremely large or extremely small numbers. All QBasic scientific notation values have a **D** or an **E** in them. The **D** represents a double-precision number; the **E**, single-precision. Why they didn't use **S** for single-precision is one of the world's greatest mysteries.

Here are some values in scientific notation:

3.65E+4   -756.423D+265   -9.1E-2   -122325.6433D-101

To find out exactly what value is represented by a number in scientific notation, take the number to the left of the **E** or **D** and multiply it by 10 raised to the number on the right of the **E** or **D**. In other words, **3.65E+4** is exactly the same as **3.65** times **104**, or **36500**.

All you have to do is move the decimal point to the left or right the number of places indicated by the rightmost digit. If the rightmost digit (the number following the **D** or **E**) has a plus sign, move the decimal to the right, and if the number has a minus sign, move the decimal to the left.

Older versions of BASIC didn't support numeric suffixes, so you could not distinguish between the different numeric data types. All numbers and variables were considered to be single-precision. String variables in BASIC have always used dollar signs at the ends of their names.

The previous table shows that a double-precision variable can hold a number as large as 1.79769313486231 multiplied by 10 followed by 308 zeros!

Code Example

```
n% = 55           ' Integer
weight! = 165.75     ' Single-precision
salary = 1987.23     ' Single-precision
atomicWeight# = -0.0000022233333#
' Double-precision
```

Code Analysis

These lines of code assign values to the different numeric data types. The first variable, **n%**, is an integer and holds the integer **55**. The second variable, **weight!**, is single-precision and holds **165.75**. The third variable, **salary**, is also single-precision. (Numeric variables without an exclamation point after their names are automatically single-precision.) The last variable, **atomicWeight#**, holds an extremely small number and is a double-precision variable.

The Least You Need to Know

☛ The goal of this chapter is to show you how to determine exactly what kind of numeric variables you are working with. The information presented here is not always considered to be the most exciting in QBasic, but you will be grateful that you now understand it when QBasic spits out a number with a trailing pound sign (#); you now know that the pound sign is just an indicator of the value's data type, namely double-precision.

☛ Reserve the use of long integer and double-precision variables for variables that need to hold extremely large or extremely small data values. For everyday values used in most games, in business, and even in scientific programs, the integer and single-precision variables work best because they are more efficient than the longer variable data types.

☛ Get comfortable with the fact that numbers and strings are called both constants and literals. They do not change (but variables can change).

☛ Use a long integer or double-precision variable suffix if you are storing extremely small or extremely large numbers.

☛ Don't store values in long integer or double-precision variables unless you need the extreme ranges they offer.

Chapter 11
What Math Can QBasic Do? Use Numeric Functions to Find Out

In This Chapter

- The integer functions
- Timing yourself
- Randomizing
- Some really hard functions

Are you thinking, "Oh no, not more math!"? Well, fear not, because this chapter makes QBasic do all the work. QBasic is a programming language that can perform simple calculations and complex calculations—all you have to do is type the correct name for the routine you want performed. This chapter is the last of the math-oriented chapters in the book. Programming computers is not for math experts—programming computers is for anybody.

QBasic supplies many built-in *functions*. A function is the term given to routines inside the QBasic language that calculate and manipulate data. The only reason that functions are not called commands is because of their nature. Commands control a program's execution, whereas functions convert values into other values.

Some of the functions described here do require trigonometric or scientific skills to understand, but you can safely skip those. Only the programmers who need them have to understand them.

All QBasic functions have names, and most of them end with parentheses. You have already seen one function in this book: **TAB()**. **TAB()** takes the value inside its parentheses (called the *argument*) and sends the cursor to that column position on the screen.

The Integer Functions

There are several built-in functions that return the integer portion of their arguments. In other words, if you put a double-precision value inside these functions' parentheses, they compute the integer portion of the number. The easiest function to learn is **INT()**, which returns the integer portion of a number. The following statement stores a **12** in **ans**:

ans = INT(12.4445533)   ' Stores a 12 in ans

You can also print the value of a function. This next statement prints a **12** on-screen:

PRINT INT(12.4445533)   ' Prints a 12

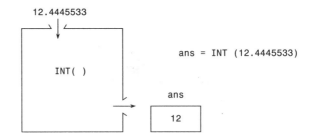

INT() is like a magic box that accepts an argument and returns an integer value based on that argument.

INT() does not round. INT() was written to return the closest integer *smaller* than the argument. This means that if you pass **INT()** a negative number, **INT()** returns the *next smallest* integer, which will be the next lowest negative number. The following example prints a **-6** because **-6** is the closest integer that is smaller than **-5.4**:

PRINT INT(-5.4)   ' Prints -6

QBasic supplies two other similar functions, **FIX()** and **CINT()**. These functions both convert their arguments to integers differently than does **INT()**. **FIX()** *truncates* its fractional portion. *Truncate* is a fancy word meaning that whatever is to the right of the whole value is chopped off; for example, **-5.4** becomes **-5** and **6.4** becomes **6**.

A function is like a box in that you put something into the top of it and something else comes out the bottom. The figure shows you what the **INT()** function's box would look like.

CINT() (for *convert integer*) does round the way you would expect. **CINT()** rounds the value to the nearest integer. Therefore, the following example prints **-6**, **5**, and **6**:

```
PRINT CINT(-5.8)      ' Prints -6
PRINT CINT(5.4)       ' Prints 5
PRINT CINT(5.5001)    ' Prints 6
```

Because the argument you want converted might be a large value whose integer portion requires a long integer result, QBasic supplies yet another function, called **CLNG()** (for *convert long*). This function converts its argument to a long integer. The following example stores **12345678** (an integer too large to fit in a regular integer variable) in **longNum&**:

A function's argument can be a constant or a variable.

```
longNum& = CLNG(12345678.345432784#)
```

Timing Yourself

QBasic supplies an interesting function that is one of the few functions which do not take parentheses because you do not pass an argument. The **TIMER** function returns the number of seconds since your computer's internal clock struck midnight.

You might wonder why you would ever need to know how many seconds have elapsed since midnight. Suppose you were timing an event. You might want to ask the user a question and decide how long it took the user to answer. You can save the value of **TIMER** before you ask the user, then subtract that value from the value of **TIMER** *after* the user answers. The difference is the number of seconds the user took to answer. Here is a program that does just that:

```
Program that times the user's response
CLS
before = TIMER     ' Save the time before asking
INPUT "What is 20 + 35"; ans
after = TIMER      ' Save the time after answering
diff = after - before
PRINT "It took you only"; diff; "seconds to answer!"
END
```

Randomizing

There is a way to make computers generate different answers with the very same program! You might wonder why you would ever need to do that, but think about game programs for a moment. If the slot machine in the back of the book always produced the same set of slot pulls every time you played the game, the game would be boring, wouldn't it? QBasic contains the **RND()** function to return a random number.

Before using **RND()**, you should use the **RANDOMIZE** statement. **RANDOMIZE** *seeds the random-number generator.* This means that a value you supply with the **RANDOMIZE** command acts as a trigger for a new set of random values. If you supply a different **RANDOMIZE** value every time you run a program, the program's **RND()** function returns a different set of values each time.

Here is the format of **RANDOMIZE**:

RANDOMIZE *seedValue*

Most of the time, QBasic programmers use the **TIMER** function in place of a *seedValue* like this:

RANDOMIZE TIMER

Because your computer's internal clock is different every time you run a program, you will produce truly random numbers after seeding the random-number generator with **TIMER**. This is the method used by the slot-machine program in Chapter 29. After you **RANDOMIZE** the random-number generator, the **RND()** function will produce random results.

RND() always returns a random number from 0 to 1. Here is some code that prints three random numbers on-screen each time you run it:

```
RANDOMIZE TIMER     ' Seed the internal random generator
PRINT RND
PRINT RND
PRINT RND
END
```

If you want something else, such as a number from 1 to 6 as you would get when simulating a dice roll, you can perform a little calculation like this:

```
PRINT INT(RND * 6) + 1
        ' Ensure the random number is from 1 to 6
```

Some Really Hard Functions

This section briefly explains the trigonometric and scientific functions that QBasic supplies. Glance through them and remember they are here. If you ever need these functions, you can come back here for guidance, but if you don't think you will, you are safe to skip them.

The table lists the remaining built-in math functions discussed in this book. After you are through, you can take a break. The next chapter describes many of QBasic's string functions, which are fun even for nontechnical people.

Mathematicians have tons of formulas they can apply to a computer's random-number sequence to see how statistically random they (the numbers, not the mathematicians!) are.

Some of QBasic's Other Math Functions

Function	Description
ABS()	Returns the positive equivalent (absolute value) of whatever value you pass it.
ATN()	Computes the arc tangent of the argument in radians.
COS()	Computes the cosine of the argument in radians.
EXP()	Computes the base of the natural logarithm (also known by mathematicians as *e*) raised to the power specified by the argument.
LOG()	Computes the natural logarithm of the function's argument.
SIN()	Computes the sine of the argument in radians.
SQR()	Computes the square root of its argument.
TAN()	Computes the tangent of the argument in radians.

TECHNO NERD TEACHES...

If you want to specify a trig function's argument in degrees rather than in radians, you can do so. Multiply the degree value by 3.141592654 (the approximate value of *pi*), and then divide that by 180. If you want to get the arc tangent of 90 degrees, the following statement does just that:

ac90 = ATN(90 * 3.141592654 / 180)

Code Example

```
PRINT "The number of seconds since midnight is"; TIMER
PRINT "You likely know that 6.7777 rounded up is"; CINT(6.777)
PRINT "How old are you"; age
RANDOMIZE age
    ' Seed the random-number generator on the user's age
PRINT "Here's a random number:"; RND
PRINT "The number of seconds since midnight now is"; TIMER
```

Code Analysis

The program first prints the number of seconds since midnight using the **TIMER** function. **TIMER** is nice to use (as is done here) to show the beginning and ending times of a program to see how long the program takes to run. Also, you can divide the value returned by TIMER to arrive at hours and minutes if you need to.

The **CINT()** function rounds values the way you would expect: The numbers round up or down to the nearest integer.

Before using a random number from **RND**, you might first want to seed the random-number generator with a value (the **TIMER** value is usually different enough to use) so that a different **RND** value is generated every time you call the **RND** function. This program uses the user's age to seed the random-number generator before printing a random number. If the same age is entered every time this program is run, the same random number will appear.

The Least You Need to Know

☛ The goal of this chapter is to show you how to streamline your routines by using some of QBasic's built-in math functions. There are integer functions that round numbers to integers in different ways, a random function that returns a random number, and a timer function (appropriately named **TIMER**) that returns a value based on your PC's internal clock.

☛ Depending on your needs, you might want to use some of the more complicated scientific and trigonometric functions too.

☛ Use the built-in math functions instead of writing your own code to do the same thing.

continues

continued

☞ Use **TIMER** when you want to time any event within your program, such as the user's response time to a question.

☞ Don't confuse **INT()**, **CINT()**, **CLNG()**, and **FIX()**. These functions seem to do the same things, but they sometimes return slightly different integer values.

☞ To produce truly random values, place a **RANDOMIZE TIMER** statement at the top of any program that uses **RND()**. The program then produces a different set of random numbers each time you run it.

☞ Don't feel as if you have to master all the math functions at once. If you don't need the trig functions, you can safely skip them.

Chapter 12

Can QBasic Do Much with Strings? Check Out QBasic's Built-In String Functions

In This Chapter

- A different case
- Trimming strings
- Talking ASCII
- Length of data
- Getting the date and time

QBasic is known as one of the best programming languages for string manipulation. Although QBasic is often touted as a *beginner's language* (it is, but it's good for pros too), QBasic excels over C, Pascal, FORTRAN, and the other languages when it comes to working with strings. The primary reason that QBasic is so string-strong is because of the built-in string-manipulation functions described in this chapter.

Most of QBasic's string functions take a string as their argument, and return a string based on that argument. Most of QBasic's string function names end with a dollar sign, indicating that they return strings.

A Different Case

QBasic includes two built-in string functions that convert from uppercase to lowercase and vice versa. A short example will demonstrate their usage. The following lines contain code that assigns two strings, each containing both uppercase and lowercase letters, to variables. Both variables are passed through the **UCASE$()** and **LCASE$()** functions. **UCASE$()** converts its string argument to all uppercase letters, and **LCASE$()** converts its string argument to lowercase letters.

```
first$ = "Example #1 of a STRing."
second$ = "Example #2 of a STRing."
newFirst$ = UCASE$(first$)
newSecond$ = LCASE$(second$)
PRINT newFirst$
PRINT newSecond$
```

Here is the output from the code:

```
EXAMPLE #1 OF A STRING.
example #2 of a string.
```

Notice that both **UCASE$()** and **LCASE$()** ignore any characters that are not alphabetic.

UCASE$() leaves uppercase letters unchanged, and LCASE$() leaves lowercase letters unchanged.

Trimming Strings

QBasic continues the long-standing BASIC tradition of providing three functions that return the left, right, and middle portions of strings. These three function names are **LEFT$()**, **RIGHT$()**, and **MID$()**. The **LEFT$()** and **RIGHT$()** functions are the easiest to use because they take fewer arguments than **MID$()**.

LEFT$() returns the left portion of a string, and **RIGHT$()** returns the right portion of a string. For example, assume that you assign the letters **ABCDEFG** to a string like this:

```
letter$ = "ABCDEFG"
```

You can print various portions of the left part of the string with **LEFT$()**. The remarks to the right of the following **PRINT** statements describe what gets printed.

```
PRINT LEFT$(letter$, 1)      ' Prints A
PRINT LEFT$(letter$, 2)      ' Prints AB
PRINT LEFT$(letter$, 3)      ' Prints ABC
PRINT LEFT$(letter$, 6)      ' Prints ABCDEF
PRINT LEFT$(letter$, 22)     ' Prints ABCDEFG
```

The second argument of **LEFT$()** indicates how much of the left part of the string you want the function to return. If you like, you can assign the left part of a string to another string variable like this:

```
firstName$ = LEFT$(fullName$, 5)
```

RIGHT$() is easy because it works just like **LEFT$()** except that it returns the rightmost portion of strings. The following **PRINT** statement prints **FL**:

If the second argument of **LEFT$()** is longer than the string itself (as in the last of the preceding five **PRINT** statements), QBasic does not display an error but simply returns the entire string.

```
city$ = "Miami, FL"
PRINT RIGHT$(city$, 2)       ' Prints FL
```

The **MID$()** function returns the middle of a string. You must give **MID$()** three arguments because **MID$()** must know where to begin pulling out characters from a string and how many to pull. Here is the format of **MID$()**:

```
MID$(string, start [, length])
```

Here is a program that shows you how to print *substrings* (portions of a string) from a longer string:

```
' Illustrates the MID$() function
CLS
words$ = "Rome Venice Florence Verona Milan"
PRINT "Italian cities to visit:"
PRINT MID$(words$, 1, 4)     ' Prints Rome
PRINT MID$(words$, 6, 6)     ' Prints Venice
PRINT MID$(words$, 13, 8)     ' Prints Florence
```

```
PRINT MID$(words$, 22, 6)    ' Prints Verona
PRINT MID$(words$, 29, 5)    ' Prints Milan
END
```

If you do not specify a *length*, QBasic returns the entire string to the right of the **start** position.

The figure makes the three substring functions even clearer by showing you how they would work on a single string.

You can see a good use of a couple of these string functions in Chapter 29's slot-machine game. Early in the game, the player has the option of continuing (by pressing **Enter**) or stopping by typing **STOP**. The program converts the user's input to uppercase, and then checks the leftmost character in the string by combining **UCASE$()** and **LEFT$()** with this line:

IF (UCASE$(LEFT$(ent$, 1)) = "S") THEN

You'll learn about **IF** in the next chapter. The combined use of **UCASE$()** and **LEFT$()** is the important point right now.

Using the LEFT$(),
MID$(), and
RIGHT$() string
functions.

LEFT$ (m$,8)   RIGHT$ (m$ (X3) ,9)

m$ = "The rain in Spain needs to drain."

WID$ (m$, 13, 5)

Talking ASCII

You will find an ASCII table in the back of the book. *ASCII* (pronounced *ask-ee*—so if you want to *know-ee* you can just hop to the table and *ask-ee*) is a code that maps a different number to each character that your computer can produce. (The first 31 ASCII codes represent *nonprintable characters,* which are codes that control computer operations such as form feeding a new page on your printer.)

Not all the ASCII table's characters appear on your keyboard. You might need to produce one of the characters that is not on your keyboard. For instance, you might want to print the symbol listed at position 172 in the ASCII table (a one-fourth symbol). To do so, use the **CHR$()** function. Put the ASCII code inside the parentheses, and QBasic returns that ASCII's symbol. The following line prints the one-fourth symbol:

PRINT CHR$(172)

The **ASC()** function does just the opposite. **ASC()** takes a string argument and returns the ASCII code for the first character in that string. The following line assigns the number **67** to the variable named **ascCode** because 67 is the ASCII value for the letter *C*:

ascCode = ASC("C")

Length of Data

The **LEN()** function works with both numbers and strings. **LEN()** returns the number of characters of memory needed to store its argument. For instance, the string **QBasic** takes six memory locations because there are six characters in **QBasic**. Therefore, **n** is assigned a **6** in this statement:

You will use **CHR$()** much more often than **ASC()**, because you will often need to print and work with characters that aren't on your keyboard.

n = LEN("QBasic")

To find out how much memory a number takes, use the number in **LEN()** like this:

N# = 23.3#
PRINT "Double-precision numbers take"; LEN(N#); " locations."

Getting the Date and Time

Perhaps two of the easiest functions are **DATE$** and **TIME$**. It doesn't take a nuclear chemist to figure out that these functions return the date and time, respectively. Unlike most of QBasic's string functions, **DATE$** and **TIME$** don't require arguments, so they do not use parentheses. The following statements print the date and assign the time to a variable:

If your computer's internal clock is not set properly, **DATE$** and **TIME$** won't return correct values.

PRINT "The date is "; DATE$ ' Might print The date is 12-18-95
t$ = TIME$ ' Might assign 16:23:55 to t$

The time is returned in the 24-hour military clock time of your computer. Therefore, any hour past 12:00 noon will be greater than 12. The time assigned to **t$** in the preceding code would be 4:23 in the afternoon (the seconds are 55).

The time had to be assigned to a string variable because both **DATE$** and **TIME$** return the date and time as strings.

Code Example

```
PRINT "Your first initial is "; LEFT$(nam$, 1)
PRINT "The last letter in your name is "; RIGHT$(nam$, 1)
PRINT "Your first letter's ASCII code is"; ASC(LEFT$(nam$, 1))
PRINT "In uppercase, your name looks like "; UCASE$(nam$)
PRINT "In lowercase, your name looks like "; LCASE$(nam$)
PRINT "Set your clock; the time is "; TIME$
```

Many large computers (called *mainframes*) use an internal EBCDIC (pronounced ebb-sid-ic) table that is very similar to the PC's ASCII table. The two tables are similar but not the same, which leads to some interesting problems when you run some PC program code on a mainframe or vice versa.

Code Analysis

These lines of code use many of the functions taught in this chapter. The string used in most of the functions is the user's name. The **PRINT** statements before each function call describe exactly what is being done in the corresponding function calls. Notice that the fourth line in the program uses an embedded function call (called a *nested function call*). The user's first initial is picked off the nam$ string, and the ASCII code for that letter is then printed.

The Least You Need to Know

☞ The goal of this chapter is to extend your knowledge of built-in functions by showing you some of QBasic's string functions. The string functions are some of the richest in any programming language. Most languages play catch-up to QBasic when it comes to string manipulation.

☞ You learned how to retrieve parts of a string and convert strings to uppercase and lowercase letters. The ASCII table also helps QBasic programmers print characters that don't even appear on the computer's keyboard.

☞ The **TIME$** and **DATE$** functions enable you to get the computer's current time and date when needed. Often, programmers like to print the date and time at the top of a report to show exactly when the report was printed.

☞ Use the built-in string functions to access and manipulate string data.

☞ Convert from uppercase to lowercase and back again with **UCASE$()** and **LCASE$()**.

☞ Return parts of a string with **LEFT$()**, **RIGHT$()**, and **MID$()**.

☞ Use **CHR$()** and the ASCII table to produce characters from your programs that aren't on your keyboard.

☞ Don't expect a.m. or p.m. times with **TIME$**. **TIME$** returns a 24-hour time.

Move along; nothing else to see here.

Chapter 13

How Does QBasic Make Decisions? With Relational Operators

In This Chapter

- ☛ IF true **THEN** do it!
- ☛ Understanding the relation
- ☛ Otherwise, use **ELSE**
- ☛ The **AND** and **OR** operators

It is possible to write extremely smart QBasic programs. Of course, being smart doesn't mean that your computer can think on its own. Computers cannot think, but they can make decisions if you teach them how to do so. You must use decision-making operators and statements if you want QBasic to make decisions.

You would want QBasic to make decisions so that the programs you write will be more beneficial to you. QBasic can look at data inside variables and determine a course of action based on statements in the program. For example, if a certain sales level is not met, you might want your QBasic program to print an exception report. If the sales level is exceeded, you might want a completely different set of statements to execute, perhaps to print a congratulatory message or to add bonus pay to the sales staff's paychecks.

This chapter begins to show you how to instruct QBasic to execute one part or another part of your programs. Until now, QBasic executed each statement in the program, one line after another. Before you are through with this chapter, you'll know how to instruct QBasic to ignore a section of your program if the data warrants it.

IF True THEN Do It!

The **IF** statement is QBasic's decision statement. Most programming languages offer an **IF** statement, and QBasic is no exception. The **IF** statement is the first QBasic statement you've seen that spans more than one line of a program. Here is the format of **IF**:

> IF *relation* **THEN**
>   *Block of one or more QBasic statements*
> **END IF**

The multiple-line **IF** always ends with the **END IF** statement. The **Block** of statements that goes between **IF** and **END IF** might contain one or many statements.

The ***Block*** of statements might or might not execute, depending on the ***relation***. Before studying what the ***relation*** means, consider this idea: The designers of QBasic didn't set out to design QBasic to be hard to use. They designed QBasic to be easy. The **IF** works just as it does in spoken language. For instance, think about how this spoken statement works:

"If the password is correct, you can go into the room."

The spoken *if* determines whether the remaining statement is allowed. The QBasic **IF** determines whether the **Block of one or more QBasic statements** executes.

Understanding the Relation

To understand the ***relation***, you have to learn six more QBasic operators, known as the *relational operators*. (Sometimes the relational operators are known as the *conditional operators,* and sometimes the ***relation*** is known as a *condition.*) The following table lists the six relational operators, and gives an example **IF** statement for each operator.

The Relational Operators

Operator	Description	Example
>	Greater than	**IF sales > 1200 THEN**
<	Less than	**IF salary < 400.50 THEN**
>=	Greater than or equal to	**IF (bonus >= expected) THEN**
<=	Less than or equal to	**IF age <= MinAge THEN**
=	Equal to	**IF (score = highScore) THEN**
<>	Not equal to	**IF answer$ <> "YES" THEN**

Suppose your program needs to ask the user how many sales calls were made that day. If the user made more than 10 sales calls, you want the program to congratulate the effort. If 10 or fewer sales calls were made, you want the program to continue without doing anything extra. In other words, *if the number of sales calls was greater than 10, print a message.* That statement translates directly into the following code:

Notice that the *relation* is often enclosed in parentheses, but the parentheses are not required.

```
INPUT "How many sales calls did you make today"; numCalls
IF (numCalls > 10) THEN
  BEEP
  PRINT "Wow, good job!  You are working hard!"
END IF
' Rest of program would follow
```

The program beeps and congratulates the salesperson if the number of sales calls was more than 10.

If the *relation* is false, the statement following **IF** does not execute. Therefore, if the number of sales calls was 10 or less, the user never knows about the congratulatory message. The **IF** has forced certain lines of code to execute only if a given condition is true.

It is fine to use strings on either side of the relational operators. QBasic uses an ASCII table like the one in the back of this book to determine whether one string is less than another (notice that uppercase letters come before lowercase, so **Tucson** would compare less than **tuba**). Here is a program that asks the user a question about a new baby:

```
INPUT "Is your baby a girl"; ans$
IF (ans$ = "yes") THEN
    PRINT "I bet she's cute!"
END IF
```

The indention after IF and ELSE is not required because QBasic is a free-form language. However, indenting the lines of code that form the two legs of an IF-ELSE statement helps each set stand apart and makes debugging easier.

Otherwise, Use ELSE

The **IF** statements you have seen have been called *single-leg* **IF** statements. In other words, you have decided what code will execute if the **relation** is true. What, however, if you want one of *two* sets of statements to execute depending on the data being tested? In the **IF** right before this section, nothing prints if the baby is a boy. You might want to print one message if the baby is a girl and another if the baby is a boy. Do you think the following code will accomplish that?

```
INPUT "Is your baby a girl"; ans$
IF (LCASE$(ans$) = "yes") THEN
    PRINT "I bet she's cute!"
END IF
PRINT "He'll be a handsome sports star some day!"
```

This **IF** does not fix anything! If the baby is a boy, the boy's message prints. However, if the baby is a girl, *both* the girl's and the boy's messages print! Remember that when the **END IF** is over, the rest of the program executes line-by-line as usual.

What if the answer is **YES** (in uppercase letters)? The **IF** would compare false, because to a computer, uppercase letters are different from lowercase (the ASCII table tells us so). You learned in the preceding chapter how to fix this potential problem. Use **LCASE$()** like this:

```
INPUT "Is your baby a girl"; ans$
    IF (LCASE$(ans$) = "yes") THEN
        PRINT "I bet she's cute!"
    END IF
```

ELSE is optional, as the brackets in the format indicate. However, when you want to specify two sets of relational code, **ELSE** is needed.

You can add the **ELSE** keyword to an **IF** statement whenever you want to specify two sets of code. The first set executes if the *relation* is true, and the other executes if the *relation* is false. Here is the complete format of **IF** with the **ELSE** keyword:

```
IF relation THEN
    Block of one or more QBasic statements
[ELSE
    Block of one or more QBasic statements]
END IF
```

Many teachers and books make too much out of the **ELSE** and confuse QBasic students, when **ELSE** is actually straightforward. Consider this section of code:

```
INPUT "Is your baby a girl"; ans$
IF (LCASE$(ans$) = "yes") THEN
    PRINT "I bet she's cute!"
ELSE
    PRINT "He'll be a handsome sports star some day!"
END IF
```

If the baby is a girl, the girl's message displays on-screen. If the baby is a boy, the boy's message displays. The **IF-ELSE** is an extremely readable statement. Here is a written description (often called *pseudocode* or *false code*) of the **IF** statement you just saw:

Ask whether the user's baby is a girl.
If the baby is a girl, print "I bet she's cute!"
otherwise, print "He'll be a handsome sports star some day!"
Continue with the rest of the program.

The AND and OR Operators

Sometimes the relational operators are not quite enough to test for all the conditions you need to test for. You can combine two relational operators together with the **AND** and **OR** keywords. As with **ELSE**, **AND** and **OR** read a lot like their spoken counterparts. Consider this code:

```
IF (inventoryTotal > 35000) AND (numSalespeople < 4) THEN
    PRINT "Hire more salespeople!"
END IF
' Rest of program would go here
```

Not all the snippets of code presented throughout these chapters comprise a complete program. It is assumed that statements would appear before and after the code presented. Only enough of the code is given at a time to zero in on the command or function being described.

If the total dollar amount of the inventory (stored in **inventoryTotal**) is more than $35,000 and if the number of salespeople on the staff (stored in **numSalespeople**—see how descriptive variable names help you understand programs faster?) is less than four, the program prints a message. In other words, the message prints only if *both* of the *relation*s on either side of **AND** are true. If either is false, the message does not print.

If the **OR** keyword had been used rather than **AND**, a different **IF** would have taken place. The code

```
IF (inventoryTotal > 35000) OR (numSalespeople < 4) THEN
    PRINT "Hire more salespeople!"
END IF
' Rest of program would go here
```

AND and OR are actually operators. They are called the *logical operators,* or the *compound relational operators.*

prints the message if *either* the inventory total is less than $35,000 *or* the number of sales people is less than four. An **OR** condition is more likely to test true than an **AND** condition, because only one side of **OR** has to be true for the entire **IF**'s *relation* to be true.

Code Example

```
INPUT "Are you a local or visitor (L or V)"; ans$
ans$ = UCASE$(ans$) ' Convert the user's response to uppercase
IF (ans$ = "L") THEN
    PRINT "You get in free because you pay state taxes!"
    PRINT "Go on in."
ELSE
    PRINT "Welcome to our state! We'd like to welcome you"
    PRINT "and charge you only a nominal fee for entrance."
END IF
```

Code Analysis

The program first asks the user to indicate a home-state location. The user enters either an L or a V according to the user's status. Just in case the user types a lowercase letter, the second line in the program converts the letter to uppercase before the **IF** takes off.

The **IF** statement then prints one of two messages depending on the user's response. This action is why **IF** helps QBasic make decisions: One or the other set of **PRINT** statements executes, but you have no idea which set will execute when you write the program. The set executed is up to QBasic when the program is run.

Chapter 29's slot-machine game uses several **IF** statements. Right before the program ends, you'll find the following **IF** statement, which prints a message depending on how much money the player loses:

```
IF (totalCash <= 0) THEN
    PRINT "Too bad. Hope you have a ticket home."
    PRINT "Come back when you've got more money."
ELSE
    PRINT "You are leaving with some money, which is more than"
    PRINT "I can say for a lot of people!  Thanks for playing!"
END IF
```

The Least You Need to Know

☛ The goal of this chapter is to show you how the **IF** statement works. You can now tell your computer to make decisions about which lines in a program to execute. The **IF** statement uses the true or false result of relational operators to see whether one set of code should execute.

☛ By adding the **ELSE** clause to the end of **IF**, you can cause one of two sets of QBasic statements to execute depending on the result of a relational test.

☛ Use **IF** to test a condition and execute certain lines of code according to the results of the test.

☛ Specify an **ELSE** section if you want one set of code or another set of code to execute depending on the result of the **IF**'s *relation*.

☛ Feel free to test strings for equality in an **IF**'s *relation* test. QBasic uses the ASCII table to determine the result of the test.

☛ Don't forget that the **THEN** keyword must follow the **IF**'s *relation*.

☛ Don't forget to convert the user's input to uppercase (with **UCASE$()**) or lowercase (with **LCASE$()**) before comparing. You never know whether the user typed the input with the Caps Lock key on.

Chapter 14

Will QBasic Work with Lots of Decisions? Learn SELECT CASE and See

In This Chapter

☛ A case for **SELECT CASE**

This chapter presents one of the hardest-looking QBasic statements in the book, **SELECT CASE**. The neat thing about **SELECT CASE**, however, is that it is really one of the easiest to use! **SELECT CASE** takes up where **IF** leaves off. By combining relational tests and the **AND** and **OR** operators, you can use **IF** to compare several relationships of data as explained in the preceding chapter. However, if you need to compare more than two or three data relationships, the **IF-ELSE** statement is too cumbersome to use.

By using **SELECT CASE**, you can cause your QBasic program to select from one of many conditions and execute certain statements accordingly. The **SELECT CASE** statement has several formats, but they all basically take on the same general look. Here is the most common (and easiest) **SELECT CASE** statement:

    SELECT CASE *expression*
    CASE *value*
       Block of one or more QBasic statements
    CASE *value*
       Block of one or more QBasic statements

[CASE *value*
    Block of one or more QBasic statements]
[CASE ELSE
    Block of one or more QBasic statements]
END SELECT

A Case for SELECT CASE

Yes, **SELECT CASE** might look difficult, but you'll see that it's a piece of cake.

In a nutshell, the **SELECT CASE** statement selects one set of statements, from several possible cases, that matches an expression. The **SELECT CASE** often replaces an **IF** within an **IF** within an **IF** (and so forth).

Perhaps the best use of **SELECT CASE** is programming a *menu* of choices. A computer menu is often useful for helping a user decide on a series of actions. You already have seen the QBasic menu system. Instead of having to remember a bunch of commands for saving a program or running a program, you only have to select from a list across the top of the screen called a menu. You can add a menu to your own programs so that your users can select from a series of things they might want to do.

Suppose you were writing a program for your banker friend who needed certain calculations done throughout the day. You might write a program that contained the following menu:

Don't concern yourself with what these calculations are all about. A banker understands them. The **SELECT CASE**, not the calculations, is our primary consideration here.

Here are your banking calculation choices:
    1. Calculate current ratio
    2. Calculate net working capital
    3. Calculate average payment period
    4. Calculate average collection period
What is your choice?

The following program would take care of the banker's needs just fine. Follow the program to see how **SELECT CASE** chooses among possible actions. If the banker's menu selection (stored in choice) is 1, the first **CASE** executes, and the other **CASE**s take care of the other possibilities:

```
CLS
' Program that performs banking analysis
PRINT "B a n k e r ' s   C a l c u l a t o r"
PRINT
PRINT "Here are your banking calculation choices:"
PRINT
PRINT " 1. Calculate current ratio"
PRINT " 2. Calculate net working capital"
PRINT " 3. Calculate average payment period"
PRINT " 4. Calculate average collection period"
PRINT
INPUT "What is your choice"; choice
PRINT
' Let the SELECT CASE decide the proper course of action
SELECT CASE choice
CASE 1:
  INPUT "What are the current assets"; ca
  INPUT "What are the current liabilities"; cl
  cr = ca / cl
  PRINT USING "& #.##"; "The current ratio is"; cr
CASE 2:
  INPUT "What are the current assets"; ca
  INPUT "What are the current liabilities"; cl
  nwc = ca - cl
  PRINT USING "& $#####,."; "The net working capital is"; nwc
CASE 3:
  INPUT "What are the accounts payable"; ap
  INPUT "What are the credit purchases"; cp
  app = (ap / cp) * 360
  PRINT USING "& ## &"; "The average payment period is";
  app; "days"
CASE 4:
  INPUT "What are the accounts receivable"; ar
  INPUT "What are the net credit sales"; ncs
  acp = (ar / ncs) * 360
  PRINT USING "& ## &"; "The average collection period is";
  acp; "days"
```

The **CASE ELSE** handles the action that takes place if the user's input does not match any of the other **CASE**s. The **CASE ELSE** is optional, but strongly recommended to take care of incorrect data.

```
CASE ELSE:
  BEEP
  PRINT "** You did not enter a correct choice **"
END SELECT
END
```

To give you an idea of how this program flows, here are two runs of the program. Trace the program listing as you follow both of them:

B a n k e r ' s   C a l c u l a t o r

Here are your banking calculation choices:

1. Calculate current ratio
2. Calculate net working capital
3. Calculate average payment period
4. Calculate average collection period

What is your choice? 3

What are the accounts payable? 2689
What are the credit purchases? 31093
The average payment period is 31 days

In the next run, the user did not enter a proper menu selection, so the **CASE ELSE** had to take over:

B a n k e r ' s   C a l c u l a t o r
Here are your banking calculation choices:
1. Calculate current ratio
2. Calculate net working capital
3. Calculate average payment period
4. Calculate average collection period
What is your choice? 6
** You did not enter a correct choice **

Code Example

```
PRINT "What would you like to order:"
PRINT "1. Italian food"
PRINT "2. Seafood"
PRINT "3. Health food"
PRINT "4. Mexican food"
PRINT "What is your choice"; ans
SELECT CASE ans
CASE 1 :
   PRINT "Our special is lasagna"
CASE 2 :
   PRINT "Our special is whiting"
CASE 3 :
   PRINT "Our special is grass root pie"
CASE 4 :
   PRINT "Our special is chili verde"
CASE ELSE :
   PRINT "What's the matter, not hungry?"
END SELECT
```

In the next chapter, you'll learn how to repeat a series of statements so that the menu reappears after a calculation has been made. The user then will not have to rerun the program to request another calculation.

Code Analysis

This **SELECT CASE** really is implementing a menu! Depending on the user's answer, one of five food messages prints. The **CASE ELSE** statement handles the condition that sometimes occurs if none of the other **CASE** values matches that of the **SELECT CASE** line. Therefore, if the user enters a **7**, the last message prints because there is no **CASE 7 :** statement.

The Least You Need to Know

- ☞ The goal of this chapter is to show you how to streamline lots of decisions into an easy-to-follow **SELECT CASE** statement. QBasic's **SELECT CASE** statement executes one of a series of statements based on a certain case matching up.

- ☞ Although you can write equivalent code using **IF-ELSE** statements inside other **IF-ELSE** statements, the **SELECT CASE** statement is easier to follow and makes your programs easier to change later if needed.

- ☞ The **SELECT CASE** is especially useful for menu selections.

- ☞ Use **SELECT CASE** to execute a set of QBasic statements based on one of several possible choices.

- ☞ Always specify a **CASE ELSE** to handle bad data that might slip into a **SELECT CASE** expression variable.

- ☞ You can use either integers or character strings for the **SELECT CASE** test expression and **CASE**s.

- ☞ Don't be thrown by the strange-looking format of **SELECT CASE**. **SELECT CASE** simply chooses from one of several sets of code based on a matching **CASE** expression.

Chapter 15

Can I Repeat Code? With the DO Loop You Can

In This Chapter

- ☞ DO a QBasic loop
- ☞ The **DO WHILE-LOOP**
- ☞ The **DO-LOOP WHILE**

This chapter teaches you how to play loop-the-loop with your QBasic programs! A *loop* is nothing more than a repeated section of a program. You often might want parts of a program to repeat, such as a menu that redisplays after each selection and a payroll program that keeps printing checks for every employee rather than just one per program run.

Loops make your programs powerful. Loops allow a section of a program to execute over and over depending on the data being processed. The only time you do not want to loop is when you accidentally write an *infinite loop*. That is a loop that never stops but keeps repeating forever.

DO a QBasic Loop

The DO statement begins a loop. There are several forms of the DO loop in QBasic. Following are the formats of two of the most common kinds of QBasic loops. The first one is called the **DO WHILE-LOOP**:

DO WHILE *relation*
  Block of one or more QBasic statements
LOOP

The next loop is called the **DO-LOOP WHILE** (notice the placement of the **WHILE**):

DO
  Block of one or more QBasic statements
LOOP WHILE relation

The *relation* looks exactly like the **IF** statement's *relation*. The **IF** and the **DO** statements have a lot in common. However, instead of performing a set of code *once* as the **IF** does if the *relation* is true, the **DO** performs a set of code many times as long as the *relation* is true. The figure shows you the action of a **DO** loop.

Part of a program repeats when a DO's relation is true.

```
                            Short program with a loop
                            A = 1
           These            DO WHILE (A < 20)
           statements          PRINT "Still counting..."
           repeat             A = A + 1
           a while          LOOP
                            PRINT "I'm ending now..."
                            END
```

The body of an **IF** statement never executes more than once. The body of a loop usually executes more than once.

The DO WHILE-LOOP

The **DO WHILE-LOOP** performs its relational test at the top of the loop. Notice that the **WHILE** *relation* appears before the body of the loop. This means that QBasic tests the *relation* before the loop ever begins, and executes the loop the first time only if the *relation* is true. Here is an example program that demonstrates this loop:

```
' Program with a loop
CLS
INPUT "Please enter a letter and I'll speak ASCII... ", ltr$
DO WHILE (ltr$ <> "")
        ' Keep looping until Enter is only keystroke
  PRINT "The ASCII value of "; ltr$; " is"; ASC(ltr$)
  PRINT "Please enter another letter ";
  INPUT "(Enter by itself ends the program) ", ltr$
LOOP
END   ' Falls through here if just Enter is pressed
```

Here is the output of the program if the user enters a letter three times and then just presses **Enter** at the fourth prompt:

```
Please enter a letter and I'll speak ASCII... a
The ASCII value of a is 97
Please enter another letter (Enter by itself ends the program) b
The ASCII value of b is 98
Please enter another letter (Enter by
itself ends the program) f
The ASCII value of f is 102
Please enter another letter (Enter by
itself ends the program)
```

The **DO WHILE**'s body continues executing as long as the *relation* is true. In this program, as long as the user enters a letter, the body of the loop prints the ASCII value of that letter

It helps to clarify where a loop begins and ends if you indent the body of **DO WHILE** loops as done here.

(with the ASC() function). When the user wants to quit, he or she can press Enter without typing a letter. An empty string (empty strings are designated with two quotation marks, "") makes the **DO WHILE** *relation* false because the *relation* is true only if the user's keystroke is *not* equal to an empty string.

The *relation* tells QBasic when to end the loop. When the *relation* is no longer true, the loop terminates and the rest of the program continues. Therefore, something inside the loop must be able to change the *relation* somehow so that the relation eventually becomes false.

You'll find a *DO WHILE* loop controlling Chapter 29's slot-machine game. The loop continues letting the player play as long as the total cash is more than $0.00.

The DO-LOOP WHILE

The **DO-LOOP WHILE** is almost like the **DO WHILE-LOOP**, with one difference: A **DO-LOOP WHILE** always executes at least once because the relation is at the bottom of the loop. The figure indicates where the two kinds of loops test for their continue/stop *relation*.

The two kinds of DO *loops test their relations at different locations.*

If you are still unsure how these two similar-but-different loops work, look at them this way: The first one might not ever execute because the *relation* might be false to begin with. The second one *always* executes at least once.

The following program uses a short number-guessing game to demonstrate the **DO-LOOP WHILE** and to bring together a lot of the concepts you have learned. The program first generates a random number. The **RANDOMIZE TIMER** ensures that the internal clock is used to seed the **RND** function so that the program is different every time you run it. A random number is then generated from 1 to 100 and stored in **rnum**. The program then loops over and over until the user guesses the number. Notice how **IF** statements inside the loop provide hints along the way. Also, the variable **count** is added to each time the user guesses incorrectly. Therefore, **count** will hold the total number of guesses the user took.

```
' Number-guessing program with count and hints
' Generates a random number for the user to guess
RANDOMIZE TIMER    ' Seed the random-number generator
rnum = INT(RND * 100) + 1  ' Generate a number from 1 to 100
count = 0
```

```
CLS
PRINT "I am thinking of a number..."
PRINT
DO
   INPUT "What number am I thinking"; userNum
   IF (userNum > rnum) THEN
        PRINT "Your guess is too high, try again"
   END IF
   IF (userNum < rnum) THEN
        PRINT "Your guess is too low, try again"
   END IF
   count = count + 1    ' Add 1 to the count
LOOP WHILE (rnum <> userNum) ' Keep looping until user guesses
PRINT "Congratulations!"
PRINT "You guessed the number in only"; count; "tries!"
END
```

Code Example

```
i = 1
DO
     PRINT "Repeating..."
     i = i + 1     ' Add 1 to i
WHILE (i <= 5)    ' Loop five times
```

Code Analysis

This section of code prints a message five times. The loop's control variable, **i**, changes inside the loop. If **i** were never changed from **1** to something else, the loop could never finish, because the **WHILE** would always be true.

   The **DO** loops are extremely useful for looping while conditions, such as data values being input by the user, are still true. If, however, you ever need to loop a specific number of times, there is a better way, as taught in the next chapter.

Don't just study the listing. The number-guessing game is most useful if you type it and run it yourself a few times to see how it works.

There are two more DO loops in QBasic that repeat until a certain condition is met, as opposed to repeating while a certain condition is met. If you want to use these two loops, change your WHILE statements to UNTIL statements in your DO loops. There are so many ways to loop that a person could get loopy!

The Least You Need to Know

☞ The goal of this chapter is to teach you ways to write QBasic loops. A loop repeats a series of one or more QBasic statements while a certain condition is true. The loop must contain a relational test at either the top or the bottom of the loop to end the loop after the condition becomes true.

☞ When you need to execute the same section of a program more than once, don't repeat the same lines back-to-back. Instead, use a **DO** loop.

☞ Use either the **DO-LOOP WHILE** or the **DO WHILE-LOOP** depending on whether you want the loop to execute at least once or maybe not at all.

☞ Be sure to do something in the loop to change the relation being tested after **WHILE**, or you'll have an infinite loop on your hands!

☞ Don't confuse **IF** with the **DO** loops. They both have a relation, but the **IF** relation controls only a single set of statements, whereas the **DO** controls a repeated set of statements.

Chapter 16

How Can I Specify Better Loop Control? Using FOR

In This Chapter

☛ Cycling with **FOR**

One of the most popular loop-control statements in QBasic is the **FOR** loop. A **FOR** loop allows more control than **WHILE** loops provide. With a **FOR** loop you can specify how many times you want to loop, whereas you must continue looping as long as a condition is true with **WHILE** loops.

There is room for both kinds of loops in QBasic programs. At times, one kind fits a program's requirements better than another. For example, if you wrote a program to handle customer orders as customers purchased items from a store, you would need to use a **WHILE** loop. The program would process orders *while* customers came through the door. If 100 customers happened to buy items, the **WHILE** loop would happen to run 100 times. At the end of the day you might want to add the 100 customer purchases to get a total for the day. You could use a **FOR** loop because you would then know exactly how many times to loop.

By incrementing counter variables, you can simulate a **FOR** loop by using **WHILE**. You can also simulate a **WHILE** with a **FOR**! Therefore, the choice of loop you use ultimately depends on which loop you feel most comfortable with at the time you need one. (You saw this in the chapter-ending code of the preceding chapter.)

Cycling with FOR

The **FOR** loop is important for controlling repeating sections of code. As with **DO-LOOP** and **IF-END IF**, a **FOR** loop spans more than one line and has a closing statement that signals where the end of the **FOR** loop occurs. This ending statement is the **NEXT** statement; you never see a **FOR** without **NEXT** a few lines later. Here is the format of the **FOR** statement:

```
FOR counter = start TO end [STEP increment]
   One or more QBasic statements
NEXT counter
```

Here is a **FOR** loop that prints **Hi** five times:

```
FOR x = 1 TO 5
   PRINT "Hi"
NEXT x
```

The **STEP** *increment* is optional because it is enclosed in brackets in the **FOR** statement's format.

The body of a **FOR** loop is usually indented (as all loop bodies should be), and the body can be several statements long if you need it to be.

The first time through the loop, **x** is **1**. After the body of the loop (the **PRINT** statement) executes, **x** becomes **2** and the loop starts over again. When **x** becomes **5**, the **PRINT** executes one last time. QBasic stops when the counter variable becomes more than the end value (which is **5** in this **FOR** loop).

The reason that the loop cycles five times is that the counter variable, **x**, is first assigned a **1**, then a **2**, and so on until it is finally assigned a **5** by the **FOR** statement.

QBasic's **FOR** works just like a spoken "for each" statement (that's why it's called **FOR**!). To gradually ease you into **FOR** loops, here is a simple loop that explains the **FOR** and **NEXT** statements probably better than any other could:

```
' This program prints the numbers 1 through 10
CLS
FOR ctr = 1 TO 10
```

```
    PRINT ctr
NEXT ctr
END
```

Here is the output from the program:

```
1
2
3
4
5
6
7
8
9
10
```

Here is the same loop written as a **DO WHILE** statement:

```
ctr = 1
DO WHILE (ctr <= 10)
    PRINT ctr
    ctr = ctr + 1    ' Add 1 to ctr
LOOP
```

FOR loops don't always count up as the preceding loop did with **ctr**. Here is a **FOR** loop that counts down before printing a message:

```
FOR cDown = 10 TO 0 STEP -1
    PRINT cDown
NEXT cDown
PRINT "Blast off!"
```

Here is the output of this code:

```
10
9
8
7
```

Notice that this **WHILE** is not as easy to follow as **FOR**, yet the two loops are equivalent. **FOR** is best used when a fixed number of repetitions has to be made based on a variable's value.

The **FOR** loop automatically changes its own counter variable. When a repetition of the **FOR** loop ends, QBasic adds the increment value to the counter variable for you. If you use a **DO** loop, you have to write the adding statement yourself.

The **DO-LOOP WHILE** loop cannot substitute for the **FOR** loop because the relation test is performed *before* the body of the **FOR** loop and after the body of the **DO-LOOP WHILE**. The **DO-LOOP WHILE**'s test, as you might recall from the end of the preceding chapter, is always at the bottom of the loop.

6
5
4
3
2
1
0
Blast off!

If a FOR loop needs to count down, you must supply a negative STEP value. You don't have to supply a STEP value if the loop counts up as shown previously, unless the counting value is to be more than one.

The following **FOR** loop counts up by threes:

```
FOR i = 1 TO 22 STEP 3   ' The STEP is required!
   PRINT i      ' Prints 1, 4, 7, 10, 13, 16, 19, 22
NEXT i
```

The following code produces an interesting effect:

```
FOR outer = 1 TO 3
   FOR inner = 1 TO 5
      PRINT inner;       ' Leaves the cursor on the same line
         NEXT inner
   NEXT outer
            ' Prints 1 2 3 4 5 1 2 3 4 5 1 2 3 4 5
```

The **FOR** loop reads a lot like the way you speak in everyday life. Consider this statement:

"For each of our 45 employees, calculate the pay and print a check."

This statement leaves no room for ambiguity. There will be 45 employees, 45 pay calculations, and 45 checks printed.

If you put a **FOR** loop in the body of another **FOR** loop, you are *nesting* the loops. In effect, the inner loop executes as many times as the outer loop dictates. You might need a nested **FOR** loop if you wanted to print five lists of your top 10 customers. The outer loop moves from 1 to 5 while the inner loop prints the 10 customers.

An additional statement sometimes comes in handy when you are working with **FOR** loops. The

EXIT FOR statement quits a **FOR** loop earlier than its natural conclusion. Depending on the data, you might need to stop a FOR loop from executing to its normal completion. Suppose you wrote a program that asked the user for 20 values to average (for a teacher with 20 students, for example), but the user has only 15 values to enter when he or she runs the program (perhaps 5 students were sick). The user could enter **-99** for a trigger value to end the loop early with a statement like this:

```
IF (inputVal = -99) THEN
  EXIT FOR
END IF
```

Code Example

```
avg = 0
INPUT "How many numbers do you need to average"; n
FOR i = 1 TO n    ' Loops n times
  INPUT "Enter a number: ", num
   avg = avg + num    ' Add the number to the total
NEXT i              ' Get another number
avg = avg / n        ' Calculate average
PRINT "The average of your numbers is"; avg
END
```

Code Analysis

This program first asks the user for a number. A **FOR** loop is then set up to loop using the variable **i** as the loop's counter variable. **i** is first assigned the value **1**, then the second time through the loop **i** becomes **2**, and so on until **i** exceeds the user's number.

Each time the body of the loop (the indented statements) executes, the value of the user's newly entered number is added to a total stored in **avg**. **avg** began with **0** (at the top of the program) and continues being added to until the **FOR** loop finishes its job.

Lastly, **avg** is divided by the number of values entered by the user, and the resulting average is printed.

The Least You Need to Know

☞ The goal of this chapter is to show you how to write **FOR** loops that execute a fixed number of times. Whereas a **WHILE** loop might execute one or more times depending on the result of a relational test, a **FOR** loop executes a fixed number of times as determined by the values and expression following the **FOR**.

☞ Use a **FOR** loop when you want to increment or decrement a variable through a loop.

☞ Remember that the **FOR** loop's relational test is performed at the top of the loop.

☞ Use a nested loop if you want to loop a certain number of times.

☞ If you need to end a **FOR** loop early, use an **EXIT FOR** statement to do so.

☞ Don't forget to use **STEP** if you want the **FOR** loop to count down (or count up more than one at a time).

☞ Don't use a start value that is greater than the end value if you want to count down with **FOR**.

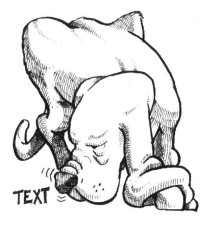

TEXT

Chapter 17

Can My Program Track Data? The READ-DATA Statements Make It Easy

In This Chapter

- ☞ READing the **DATA**
- ☞ Seeing **READ-DATA** in action
- ☞ An extra **DATA** value

As you write QBasic programs, you will find that you often initialize the same set of variables over and over in more than one program. For example, suppose you write programs for an accounting firm that has four offices located in different quadrants of your city. The offices might be distinguished in reports and on the computer screen by their locations, **East**, **West**, **North**, and **South**. In every program that deals with the four offices, you'll probably have statements that look something like this:

```
office1$ = "East"
office2$ = "West"
office3$ = "North"
office4$ = "South"
```

The assignments would be more lengthy if there were 10 different office locations rather than only 4.

Before computers got keyboards and video screens, data had to be stored on punch cards that were easy to mix up and drop.

There is lots of data, such as month names and days of the week, that you will initialize time and again in a lot of different programs. Instead of listing a bunch of assignment statements that take up program space, you can more directly store and assign these data values using **READ** and **DATA** statements.

READ and **DATA** go together—you'll never see a program with one and not the other. Unlike **FOR** and **NEXT** and **IF** and **END IF**, however, there does not have to be a one-to-one correspondence with **READ** and **DATA**. There might be one **READ** and many **DATA** statements, or the other way around.

READing the DATA

Use **READ** and **DATA** only to fill variables with values you know at the time you write the program. You cannot use **READ** to initialize a variable with user input-that is the job of **INPUT**. Here are the formats of the **READ** and **DATA** statements:

> READ variable [, variable] [, variable] [, ..., variable]

> DATA literal [, literal] [, literal] [, ..., literal]

For a review of the term *literal*, review Chapter 10, "How Do I Specify Different Data?"

There can be one or more variables following **READ**, and there can be one or more literals following **DATA**. Only variable names follow **READ** statements, but variable names never follow **DATA** statements.

If you list more than one variable or literal in a **READ** or **DATA** statement, you must separate those variables or literals with commas.

READ and **DATA** replace a long series of assignment statements. That is their only purpose. Often, it is easier to perform variable assignments using **READ** and **DATA** than using the equal sign. The accounting office assignment statements listed in this chapter's introduction can be rewritten using these **READ** and **DATA** statements:

READ office1$, office2$, office3$, office4$
DATA "East", "West", "North", "South"

The data types of the **READ** variables must match up with the literal data types after **DATA**. Here is a **READ** statement that reads both numeric and string variables. The **DATA** statement lists literals of the same data types. QBasic issues an error if you attempt to run a program in which the **DATA** types do not match the variables being read with **READ**.

The figure shows how QBasic views the following two statements:

READ age%, name$, salary#, weight!
DATA 31, "Victoria Barkley", 425553.10, 116.5

The variables after **READ** *and the values after* **DATA** *must match in number and type.*

The **DATA** can be spaced over several lines. Here is an equivalent set of statements:

READ age%, name$, salary#, weight!
DATA 31
DATA "Victoria Barkley", 425553.10
DATA 116.5

Seeing READ-DATA in Action

Typing a list of **READ** and **DATA** statements might seem like just as much work as typing several assignment statements—and it is. The advantage of **READ** and **DATA** is that all your data can be in one place and you can change it easier than if you must search through a program looking for assignment statements.

TECHNO NERD TEACHES...

DATA statements are known to be *passive*. That is, they don't actually do anything but hold data that will be read by a **READ** statement. As QBasic reads data, that data is remembered by QBasic and never read again. Therefore, data values in **DATA** statements can go anywhere in a program. Some QBasic programmers prefer to put all their **DATA** statements at the end of the program listing to get the data out of the way, even though **READ** statements appear throughout the earlier part of the program reading that data. **DATA** statements can go anywhere before, immediately after, or many lines after the **READ** statements that read the data. When QBasic encounters a **READ**, QBasic scans the program looking for *unread* **DATA** values and assigns the first one found to the variable being read next.

Here is a simple program that uses **DATA** statements to store a list of values. A loop reads those values one at a time, adding them to produce a total:

```
total = 0      ' No numbers have been added yet
FOR i = 1 TO 8
  READ num
  total = total + num   ' Add the value just read to total
NEXT i
PRINT "The total of the numbers is"; total
DATA 32, 67, 86, 34, 65, 12, 69, 10
```

The **READ** statement *will not read the same value twice.*

The following program reads five Presidents' first names into variables and then prints the names. Notice that the **DATA** statement immediately follows the **READ** statement here. It does not matter where you place a **DATA** statement.

```
' Program to read and print five names
FOR n = 1 TO 5
  READ pres$       ' Read the next name
  DATA "Thomas", "Abe", "Richard", "Ronald", "George"
  PRINT pres$
NEXT n
END
```

An Extra DATA Value

Many QBasic programmers insert an extra **DATA** value at the beginning of their **DATA** statements. The extra value is just a number that indicates how many **DATA** values follow. You can then add or remove **DATA** values without worrying about the rest of the program. For example, the following program reads 10 **DATA** values, totals them, then computes their average. Notice that the first **DATA** value, 10, is not really **DATA**, but it tells QBasic exactly how many times the **FOR** loop is to repeat.

```
' Read and compute DATA based on a count value
READ numData       ' Find out how many data values there are
total = 0          ' Nothing in total yet
FOR c = 1 TO numData
  READ dataValue
  total = total + dataValue   ' Add the data value just read
NEXT c
' Compute the average
avg = total / numData
PRINT "The average of the data is"; avg
DATA 10
DATA 4, 6, 12, 64, 40, 23, 45, 60, 19, 52
END
```

If you want to add more **DATA** values, change the first **DATA** value so that it reflects the count of the items that follow. The rest of the program still works. You truly have data that changes without having to change the program.

Code Example

```
READ checkRate
READ savRate
PRINT "The checking account rate is"; checkRate
PRINT "The savings account rate is"; savRate
DATA .07, .085
```

Code Analysis

This code reads two values into checking-account and savings-account interest rate variables. Both of the **READ** statement's values are stored in a single **DATA** statement. You don't have to have a corresponding **READ** for every **DATA** or vice versa. As long as there are enough **DATA** values following **DATA** to fill all the program's **READ** variables, the program will work fine.

The **DATA** statement could appear anywhere in the code's program, and the program would work without any different result. The data in **DATA** statements is easy to change because all the program's data appears in the same section of the program if you group your **DATA** statements together.

The Least You Need to Know

☞ The goal of this chapter is to explain **READ** and **DATA** statements. The **READ** statement reads values into variables. **READ** gets its values from **DATA** statements that appear elsewhere in the program. The command **READ** is always followed by variable names, and **DATA** is always followed by constant data values.

☞ The **DATA** statement or statements don't have to be next to their corresponding **READ** statements. **DATA** statements are passive; they don't do anything by themselves. **READ** will search for **DATA** no matter where the **DATA** statements reside in the program.

☞ Use **READ** and **DATA** to assign variables values that are known in advance.

☞ Put all **DATA** statements together (the end of program is best) to make them easier to maintain.

☞ If your **DATA** changes frequently, consider controlling the **DATA** with a count value. If you add or remove **DATA** values, you only have to change the count.

☞ Don't mix data types. **READ**ing a string value into a numeric variable is just as wrong as trying to assign a string to a numeric variable.

This page unintentionally left blank.

Chapter 18

Can QBasic Deal with Lists? Use Arrays for That

In This Chapter

- Defining arrays
- Using arrays

An *array* is a list of variables. Not just any variables, but special kinds of variables called *array variables*. Any of QBasic's data types can be turned into an array if you need to keep track of lots of values. Compared with the stand-alone variables you have read about so far, array variables are much easier to work with. You don't have to give each variable in the array list a different name. Instead, the entire array of variables has a single name.

Before getting too much further into arrays, you could use an overview: If you ever want to store lots of data, such as 100 employee names, 35 student grades, 500 inventory items, or 1,000 checks you've written over the past year, it is much easier to use an array than to use a bunch of differently named variables.

Each of the variables in an array list is called an **element**. Therefore, if you store 100 names in a string array, you simply have 100 elements, each of which is different, but all 100 elements are the same data type (strings).

Defining Arrays

When you work with several non-array variables, you have to assign each a different name. If you wrote a program to keep track of your monthly household expense total, you might use variable names such as these:

expense1   expense2   expense3   expense4   expense5

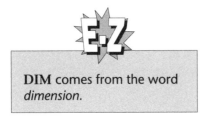

DIM comes from the word *dimension.*

Instead of keeping track of lots of variable names, you should use an array. Unlike regular variables, with an array you have to tell QBasic near the top of a program that you'll need an array. In other words, you don't have to tell QBasic that you need a variable named **expense1** because it is a regular non-array variable; you can just start using it. However, before using an array, you have to tell QBasic that you'll need one.

The **DIM** statement tells QBasic that you'll need an array later in the program. **DIM** tells QBasic the name of the array and how many elements are in it. Only after including the **DIM** can you use the array. Here is the format of **DIM**:

DIM arrayName(numElements) [, arrayName(numElements)...]

The following statement reserves eight array elements. You know the array is single-precision because all variables that have no data-type suffixes are single-precision, as you learned in Chapter 10, "How Do I Specify Different Data?" A picture of the array as it is stored in memory is shown in the figure.

DIM amounts(8)   ' Reserve 8 array elements

The eight dimensioned array elements and their subscripts.

Each array element has a *subscript,* a number in parentheses. The subscript differentiates each array element from the other array elements. Because the array elements are differentiated by a subscript value rather than a different variable name, you can use a **FOR** loop to scan through the array (printing the array, totaling it, or whatever else you might want to do with the values).

Notice that each subscript is enclosed in parentheses.

Each array element in the figure has a zero because QBasic always zeroes out all variables. Array elements are variables stored as a list.

TECHNO NERD TEACHES...

QBasic does reserve an element with the subscript 0, but most QBasic programmers start with the subscript 1 instead. Beginning the array at subscript 0 means that an array you dimension as 8 actually has 9 elements (with the subscripts 0 through 8).

Using Arrays

You will use arrays to keep track of lots of data. You can ask the user for lots of values, store those values in an array, and then print those values in any order you want. Array elements are variables that you distinguish from each other with subscripts. Following is a short program that dimensions 20 array elements, reads the numbers into the array from **DATA** statements, and then prints the array backward. Because you can reference an array in any order, the **FOR** loop prints the array backward.

```
' Reads values into an array and prints them backward
DIM vals(20)
' Read the array values
FOR i = 1 TO 20
   READ vals(i)
NEXT i
' Print the array backward
PRINT "Here is the array:"
FOR i = 20 TO 1 STEP -1
   PRINT vals(i)
NEXT i
DATA 10, 41, 34, 93, 29, 30, 73, 88, 4, 12
DATA 65, 34, 70, 41, 23, 41, 16, 52, 44, 34
END
```

BY THE WAY

Here would be a nice exercise to test your array forte: Add some code to this program that totals the array as you read each value, then prints the total after all the array elements are printed.

Suppose you wanted to write a program to keep track of a company's inventory. Although the program shown next still has room for improvement (a true inventory program needs to be able to store values in a disk file and print listings to the printer), the program presents a good start toward improving your understanding of arrays.

```
' Inventory program that uses arrays
' Room for up to 50 inventory items
DIM prodCode$(50)
DIM desc$(50)
DIM price!(50)
DIM quant%(50)
numItems = 0 ' Inventory count
```

```
' Get all the inventory items from the user
CLS
FOR numItems = 1 TO 50
  PRINT
  PRINT "What is the next product code"
  INPUT "(Press Enter to stop entering)"; prodCode$(numItems)
  IF (prodCode$(numItems) <> "") THEN
    INPUT "What is the item's description"; desc$(numItems)
    INPUT "What is the item's price"; price!(numItems)
    INPUT "What is the item's quantity"; quant%(numItems)
  ELSE
    numItems = numItems - 1 ' Don't increment count after all
    EXIT FOR
  END IF
NEXT numItems
' Print the listing on the screen
PRINT
PRINT "Here is an inventory listing:"
FOR cnt = 1 TO numItems
  PRINT
  PRINT "Product Code: "; prodCode$(cnt)
  PRINT "Description: "; desc$(cnt)
  PRINT "Price:"; price!(cnt)
  PRINT "Quantity:"; quant%(cnt)
NEXT cnt
END
```

Here is sample output from the program. Although only 3 inventory items are entered and printed here, the program's array size leaves room for up to 50.

What is the next product code
 (Press Enter to stop entering)? 1A2C-7
What is the item's description? Wedge Widgets
What is the item's price? 2.13
What is the item's quantity? 47

What is the next product code
 (Press Enter to stop entering)? 4G5S-9
What is the item's description? Bolts (small)

What is the item's price? .32
What is the item's quantity? 165

What is the next product code
 (Press Enter to stop entering)? 7T5W-0
What is the item's description? Bolts (large)
What is the item's price? .54
What is the item's quantity? 490

What is the next product code
 (Press Enter to stop entering)?

Here is an inventory listing:

Product Code: 1A2C-7
Description: Wedge Widgets
Price: 2.13
Quantity: 47

Product Code: 4G5S-9
Description: Bolts (small)
Price: .32
Quantity: 165

Product Code: 7T5W-0
Description: Bolts (large)
Price: .54
Quantity: 490

Code Example

```
DIM seasons$(4)        ' Reserve storage
FOR i = 1 TO 4
   READ seasons$(i)    ' Store a season name in the array
NEXT i
DATA "Winter"
DATA "Spring"
DATA "Summer"
DATA "Fall"
```

```
PRINT "The first season is "; seasons$(1)
PRINT "The second season is "; seasons$(2)
PRINT "The third season is "; seasons$(3)
PRINT "The fourth season is "; seasons$(4)
END
```

Code Analysis

This program reserves a four-element string array named **seasons$** that hold the names of the four seasons. The season names are read into the array using **READ** and **DATA** statements and then are printed.

With only four names, an array is not really necessary, but the seasons$ array does provide a nice storage bin for the data.

The Least You Need to Know

☞ The goal of this chapter is to teach you how to store lists of values in array variables. An array is just a list of variables. Instead of having different names, the variables in the array, called elements, are differentiated by a numeric subscript.

☞ Before you can use an array in a QBasic program, you must reserve storage for the array with a **DIM** statement. **DIM** comes from the word *dimension*.

☞ Use arrays when you want to store lots of values of the same data type.

☞ Put the array's data type suffix in front of the subscript's parentheses.

☞ Use a **FOR** loop to step through each element of your array.

☞ Don't forget to dimension enough elements for your arrays.

Recycling tip:
tear this page out and photocopy it.

Chapter 19

What About Tables of Data? QBasic Offers Matrix Control

In This Chapter

- ☞ Dimensioning arrays
- ☞ Using matrices
- ☞ Let's write a program

Some data fits better in a *matrix* than in an array. A matrix is nothing more than a *table* of values, whereas an array is just a list of values. Often, QBasic programmers call matrices *tables* rather than *matrices* because a table better describes the look of matrix data. Not all data fits in a matrix format. It might be a while before you use matrices, but they are handy when you need them.

There is very little in this chapter that you did not learn about in the preceding chapter. Matrices have subscripts. A matrix is a table of variables, and each variable is called an *element*. The table has one name, and the individual elements are differentiated by their subscripts.

The primary difference between matrices and arrays is their layout in memory. A matrix (table) has both rows and columns, and therefore each matrix element has *two* subscripts, one for the row and one for the column of the element.

The first subscript indicates the rows, and the second one indicates columns. The **myPay** matrix contains 60 elements ranging from **myPay(1,1)** to **myPay(5,12)**.

Dimensioning Arrays

Suppose you needed to write a program to keep track of your annual salary. You wouldn't need an array because there is only one value to track! However, what if you wanted to keep each month's pay stored so that you could print any or all of the amounts? An array of 12 values would be perfect for that purpose. Now, what if you wanted to keep track of *five years'* worth of those monthly payroll values? A matrix is perfect for that.

Here is the **DIM** statement that would reserve five years' worth of 12 monthly values:

DIM myPay(5, 12)   ' Reserve 5 years worth of monthly payroll

The figure shows you the table generated by this **DIM** statement. The **DIM** statement for tables always includes two subscripts, one for the rows and one for the columns.

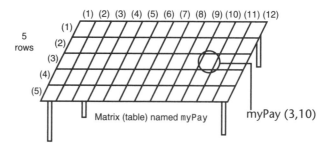

*Looking at the format of the **myPay** matrix.*

The following assignment statements put values in some of myPay's elements:

```
myPay(2, 1) = 4124.34   ' The 2nd year, 1st month
myPay(3, 5) = 2438.52   ' The 3rd year, 5th month
myPay(3, 12) = 5234.29  ' The 3rd year, 12th month
myPay(4, 6) = 6952.12   ' The 4th year, 6th month
```

Of course, instead of assigning individual matrix values, your programs will usually loop and ask the user for the values or read them from DATA (or read them from a disk file, as you'll learn how to do in the next chapter).

Using Matrices

Nested **FOR** loops are perfect for stepping through matrices. For instance, the outer loop can control the rows (in myPay, the row numbers would go from 1 to 5), and the inner loop can control the columns (in **myPay**, the column numbers would go from 1 to 12). The following section of code dimensions a matrix named **values** to 3 rows and 7 columns, then assigns a **25** to each value in the matrix. (Why you would want to do *that* is a mystery to both of us!)

```
DIM values(3, 7)
FOR rows = 1 TO 3
  FOR cols = 1 TO 7
    values(rows, cols) = 25
  NEXT cols
NEXT rows
```

> **OOPS!**
>
> Matrix variables can have data type suffixes just like any other kind of variables. The data type suffix goes just before the left parenthesis, like this: **myPay#(2, 3)** or **names$(5, 1)**.

Remember that a nested **FOR** loop is a loop within a loop. The **rows** variable steps through each row while the inner loop makes the **cols** variable step "across" each column in the row.

Using a nested **FOR** loop for initializing and printing a table might be made even clearer if you saw the **row** and **cols** variables printed as done here:

```
FOR rows = 1 TO 3
FOR cols = 1 TO 7
PRINT rows; TAB(5);          cols
NEXT cols
NEXT rows
```

Here are the first few lines of output (you can figure out the rest):

```
1   1
1   2
```

```
1  3
1  4
1  5
1  6
1  7
2  1
2  2
2  3
```

Think of these printed numbers as the table's subscripts, and you'll see why a nested loop is perfect for stepping through every element in a table.

Let's Write a Program

Perhaps a step-by-step building of a program might further explain the use of tables. Suppose you wanted to write a program that printed a report for a home mail-order business. The mail-order business sells five different sets of stationery. Because of inventory control, you want to print a report showing how each set's sales compares with the other's. The sets are named Bright Birds, Fun Flowers, Krazy Kids, Colorful Creation, and Thanx-a-Lot.

The report will be printed at the end of each month, and you'll want each week's sales printed by stationery set. In other words, the report will show a table with five columns, one column for each set of stationery. The table will have four rows, one row for each week. You can dimension the table like this:

DIM cards(4, 5)   ' 4 rows, 5 columns

Even better would be the storage of the data on disk, as you'll learn in the next chapter.

Instead of prompting the user for the 20 values every time the report is printed, the program should read the 20 values from **DATA** statements. Each month, the **DATA** statements can change so a new report is generated.

The following code would read the 20 data values for the card's sales into the table:

```
FOR week = 1 TO 4
  FOR set = 1 TO 5
    READ cards(week, set)
  NEXT set
NEXT week
DATA 425.64, 342.34, 132.67, 592.00, 352.67
DATA 294.21, 291.10, 183.93, 452.46, 368.19
DATA 381.45, 523.45, 132.30, 432.12, 425.53
DATA 317.66, 343.45, 423.54, 311.44, 685.21
```

After the data is read, it is time to print a nice-looking report. Of course, you should label the columns and rows. The following **LPRINT** statements would be perfect for the stationery set names across the top of each column:

```
LPRINT "    Bright  Fun   Krazy  Colorful  Thanx-"
LPRINT "    Birds   Flowers  Kids  Creation  a-lot"
```

In a moment you'll see why the extra space was left before the titles.

The data values now must be printed. You'll want to space the values properly so that they print under the titles. Also, the week number at the beginning of each row would be helpful. Try to figure out how the following statements would produce the data:

```
FOR week = 1 TO 4
  PRINT "Week"; week;   ' Leave a trailing cursor
  FOR set = 1 TO 5
            ' Ensure that 4 blanks print after numbers
    PRINT USING "###.##   "; cards(week, set);
  NEXT set
  PRINT   ' At end of each row, move cursor down to next line
NEXT week
```

You want **Week 1**, **Week 2**, and so on only at the *start* of each line. Therefore, those labels should print only inside the outer loop, not after the inner loop prints each number. To keep the numbers aligned, a **PRINT USING** was used. A trailing semicolon is left at the end of each value printed so that the *next* value prints on that same line. After all five columns have printed, a **PRINT** residing on a single line moves the cursor down to start the next row.

Finally, a total of each stationery set would be helpful to show which set sells the most. Only five totals are needed, one for each set. Another array of five values would be helpful here. The following code would dimension the array and total each of the five sets:

```
DIM totals(5)
totals(1) = cards(1, 1) + cards(2, 1) + cards(3, 1) + cards(4, 1)
totals(2) = cards(1, 2) + cards(2, 2) + cards(3, 2) + cards(4, 2)
totals(3) = cards(1, 3) + cards(2, 3) + cards(3, 3) + cards(4, 3)
totals(4) = cards(1, 4) + cards(2, 4) + cards(3, 4) + cards(4, 4)
totals(5) = cards(1, 5) + cards(2, 5) + cards(3, 5) + cards(4, 5)
```

If you study the subscripts being used in the totaling, you might see how a nested loop would make the totaling easier. Although the following code doesn't take a lot less typing, the nested loops do make the code easier to maintain if more weeks are needed later:

```
FOR sets = 1 TO 5
    FOR week = 1 TO 4
        totals(sets) = totals(sets) + cards(week, sets)
    NEXT week
NEXT sets
```

Putting all these pieces together produces the following program. Comments and underlining add the finishing touches. Below the program, the output is shown so that you'll be able to trace what is going on.

```
' Program that prints a report showing a mail-order stationery
' business's monthly sales, broken down by week and set
CLS
DIM cards(4, 5), totals(5)
' Read the data
FOR week = 1 TO 4
  FOR set = 1 TO 5
    READ cards(week, set)
  NEXT set
NEXT week
' Total the five sets
FOR sets = 1 TO 5
  FOR week = 1 TO 4
    totals(sets) = totals(sets) + cards(week, sets)
  NEXT week
```

Doesn't the output look nice? The table presented here is typical of many report programs. The program is a little tough, but not impossible to figure out. Spending some time learning exactly how this program operates will pay dividends later!

```
NEXT sets
' Print a report
LPRINT "      Bright   Fun   Krazy   Colorful   Thanx-"
LPRINT "      Birds   Flowers   Kids   Creation   a-lot"
FOR week = 1 TO 4
   LPRINT "Week"; week;  ' Leave a trailing cursor
   FOR set = 1 TO 5
               ' Ensure that 4 blanks print after numbers
      LPRINT USING "###.##   "; cards(week, set);
   NEXT set
   LPRINT  ' At end of each row, move cursor down to next line
NEXT week
LPRINT "      ---   ---   ---   ---   ---"
LPRINT "     ";
FOR i = 1 TO 5
   LPRINT USING "####,.##  "; totals(i);
NEXT i
DATA 425.64, 342.34, 132.67, 592.00, 352.67
DATA 294.21, 291.10, 183.93, 452.46, 368.19
DATA 381.45, 523.45, 132.30, 432.12, 425.53
DATA 317.66, 343.45, 423.54, 311.44, 685.21
END
```

Here is the program's output:

| | Bright | Fun | Krazy | Colorful | Thanx- |
	Birds	Flowers	Kids	Creation	a-lot
Week 1	425.64	342.34	132.67	592.00	352.67
Week 2	294.21	291.10	183.93	452.46	368.19
Week 3	381.45	523.45	132.30	432.12	425.53
Week 4	317.66	343.45	423.54	311.44	685.21
	---	---	---	---	---
	1,418.96	1,500.34	872.44	1,788.02	1,831.60

Code Example

```
DIM weights(3, 3) ' Reserve a matrix with 3 rows and columns
FOR month = 1 TO 3   ' The rows represent months
   FOR people = 1 TO 3  ' The columns hold people's weights
      READ (month, people)  ' Fill the matrix with weights
   NEXT people
```

```
NEXT month
DATA 135, 124, 122
DATA 189, 176, 184
DATA 120, 121, 113
```

Code Analysis

This code reads three people's weights, over a three-month period, into a matrix named weights. The matrix has three rows and three columns. Each row represents each of the three people's weights over the three month period.

Nested **FOR-NEXT** loops are useful for initializing and printing matrix variables.

The Least You Need to Know

☞ The goal of this chapter is to extend your knowledge of arrays by showing you how to reserve and use multidimensional arrays. A multidimensional array, called a matrix, has more than one subscript. The values in a matrix form a table (not just a list) that has rows and columns. You must specify two subscripts in a matrix, one for the row number and one for the column number.

☞ Use two-dimensional tables (also called *matrices*) when you have data that fits into a row-and-column format.

☞ A nested **FOR** loop is perfect when you need to step through all the elements in a matrix.

☞ Be sure to use two subscripts when you dimension a matrix.

☞ Don't confuse the QBasic *matrix* with the mathematical term *matrix*. A QBasic matrix is nothing more than an array that appears in row/column order. Nothing extra is required to work with QBasic matrices than what you already know.

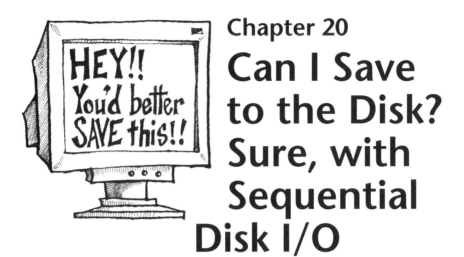

Chapter 20

Can I Save to the Disk? Sure, with Sequential Disk I/O

In This Chapter

- Types of disk access
- Opening the file drawer
- Creating a file
- Reading files
- Adding to a file

Be proud! The commands that you are learning are powerful, and the skills you are building will be well rewarded when you write programs for yourself and others. There is, however, one piece of the pie that you still need to understand: how to read from and write to disk files. The disk is semipermanent; after you write data to a disk, that data stays there until you change or delete it.

Until now, you had to either save the program's data in **DATA** statements or prompt the user with **INPUT** every time the program was run. There are drawbacks to both methods: If the data changes, you don't want the user to have to change **DATA** statements because the user of your programs knows nothing about **READ**, **DATA**, variables, and

BY THE WAY

A disk holds magnetic data just like a cassette tape. You can even store music on your disk drive with today's multimedia computers.

the like. In addition, you don't want to get calls in the middle of the night from some user wanting you to come over and change the **DATA** statements. The second method of getting data into the program, through **INPUT** statements, is still important, but after the user enters his or her data, that user doesn't want to reenter the same data every time the program is run.

The solution is to use disk files. After you get data from the user with **INPUT** statements, you can save the data to the disk. Other programs can then read that data from the disk and print or change it as needed. The figure helps show the importance of disk files to the long-term storage of your data.

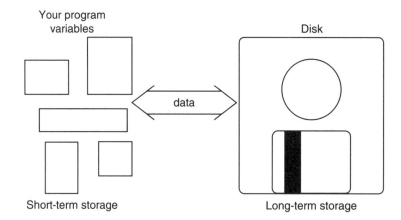

Your program variables

Disk

data

Short-term storage

Long-term storage

You can make your short-term variables last by storing them on disk.

Another advantage that random-access files have over sequential-access files is that you can change random-access files without re-creating the entire file. If you want to change a sequential-access file, you must rewrite the entire file with the new change and delete the old file.

Types of Disk Access

There are two methods QBasic uses to store data on disks: *sequential access* and *random access*. This chapter explores sequential access. The difference between the two methods is this: Sequential-access files must be read in the same order in which they were written to. Not all data fits within a sequential file. For instance, a history of sales would make a good sequential file because the data would be stored in the file in the order the sales were made. However, a parts inventory would not make good sequential file data because you want to be able to access any part in the inventory regardless of when the item was entered in the inventory.

Opening the File Drawer

Before you can read from or write to a file, you must open the file. When you are done with a disk file, you must close the file. Opening the file attaches a *filenumber* to a filename. After you open a file and attach that number, you will then use the number rather than the filename in the rest of the program.

Opening a disk file is analogous to opening a file cabinet drawer. You must open the drawer before you can access a file in the cabinet. You must open a disk file before you can access it. Always close a disk file when you no longer need to access it, or QBasic might lose some of the last few characters you wrote to the disk. (You should close the cabinet drawer when you are done with it too, or you might hit your head!)

Opening and closing disk files actually causes QBasic to do a lot of work behind the scenes. When you open a file, QBasic makes sure there is room on the disk and in the disk directory for the file. QBasic also makes sure that the filename you specify is valid and does some other important disk housekeeping chores, as well as error-checking. Closing disk files forces QBasic to write the last remaining data to the disk (the data might be stored in a memory *buffer*, or temporary holding area until you close the file) and update the disk directory.

Here is the format of the **OPEN** statement:

OPEN filename$ FOR mode AS [#]filenumber

The *filename$* is a string containing a valid filename. If you understand drives and directories, you can specify a complete pathname before the filename. The **mode** is a value from the table that shows sequential mode values. The *filenumber* (notice that the pound sign is optional) is a number from **1** to **255** that you attach to an open file.

If you open three files, you'll probably use **1**, **2**, and **3** for the three files in their corresponding **OPEN** statements.

Table 20.1   The QBasic Sequential Mode Values

Mode	Description
OUTPUT	Used for writing data to a file. If the file already exists, QBasic overwrites the file. If the file does not exist, QBasic creates the file.
APPEND	Used for adding (*appending*) data to a file. If the file already exists, QBasic directs the output from your program to the end of the file. If the file does not exist, QBasic creates the file.
INPUT	Used for reading data from a file. The file you are opening to read should first exist. If the file does not exist when you attempt to open it for input, QBasic issues an error message.

Suppose you wanted to create a sequential file to store your checkbook data. Here is an **OPEN** statement that would do so:

OPEN "checks.dat" FOR OUTPUT AS #1

If you wanted to add to the check file, you would write an **OPEN** statement that looked like this:

If other files were open when you opened the **checks.dat** file, you would pick a different **filenumber** if the **1** was already taken by another open file in the program.

OPEN "checks.dat" FOR APPEND AS #1

To read the file in a program, you would open it like this:

OPEN "checks.dat" FOR INPUT AS #1

Closing files is easy. Here is the format of the **CLOSE** statement:

CLOSE [[#]*filenumber*] [, ..., [#]*filenumber*]

You can close a file attached to *filenumber* 1 like this:

CLOSE #1

You can close three files, each attached to the first three *filenumbers*, in a single **CLOSE** like this:

> **CLOSE #1, #2, #3**

Creating a File

The **WRITE #** statement is a perfect statement to use for writing to a sequential disk file. **WRITE #** writes both string and numeric variables to a disk file, putting quotation marks around string data and separating all the data values in the file with commas. This makes the data easy to read with a mirror-image **INPUT #**. Here is the format of **WRITE #**:

> **WRITE #***filenumber data* [*..., data*]

And here is the format of **INPUT #**:

> **INPUT #***filenumber data* [*..., data*]

Following is a program that writes some words and numbers to the disk:

You can specify the filename in either uppercase or lowercase letters.

```
' If you don't have a hard disk, change the C:
' to another drive
OPEN "c:\outfile.dat" FOR OUTPUT AS #1
WRITE #1, "Michael W.", 14, 87.5
WRITE #1, "Mary C.", 15, 94.1
WRITE #1, "Jack R.", 13, 76.7
CLOSE #1   ' Always close a file when you are done
END
```

Here is a listing of the disk file created with this program:

> **"Michael W.",14,87.5**
> **"Mary C.",15,94.1**
> **"Jack R.",13,76.7**

Reading Files

Reading a sequential data file that you created is almost as easy as writing it. There is only one additional job you must take care of. Most of the time,

Yes, **-1** is a strange return value, but that's the way **EOF()** works. The next program shows you how to read a sequential file and stop when you get to the end of the file.

you'll set up a loop to read values from a file and print or process the values as you read them. Unless you know exactly how many records a file contains, you run the risk of reading past the end of the file.

QBasic supplies the **EOF()** function, which becomes true if you just read the end of the file. **EOF()** requires the filenumber of the file you are reading in **EOF()**'s parentheses. **EOF()** returns a -1 if the end of the file is reached.

```
' If you don't have a hard disk, change the
' C: to another drive
CLS
' Print titles on the screen
PRINT "Name"; TAB(16); "Age"; TAB(31); "Score"
OPEN "c:\outfile.dat" FOR INPUT AS #1
' Read and print until you reach the end of file
DO
   INPUT #1, name$, age, score
   PRINT name$; TAB(15); age; TAB(30); score
LOOP WHILE EOF(1) <> -1    ' EOF(1) returns -1 at end-of-file
CLOSE #1 ' Always close a file when you are done
END
```

Here is the output from the program:

Name	Age	Score
Michael W.	14	87.5
Mary C.	15	94.1
Jack R.	13	76.7

Adding to a File

If you want to add to the end of a sequential file, you can do so by using the **APPEND** file access keyword. After you open a file for **APPEND**, subsequent **WRITE #** statements add data to the file. The following program adds two names to the data file created and read in the previous sections:

```
' If you don't have a hard disk, change the
' C: to another drive
CLS
OPEN "c:\outfile.dat" FOR APPEND AS #1  ' Adds to end of file
WRITE #1, "Linda P.", 13, 80.3
WRITE #1, "Ron H.", 14, 99.1
CLOSE #1   ' Always close a file when you are done
END
```

Here is the file after the new lines are added:

```
"Michael W.",14,87.5
"Mary C.",15,94.1
"Jack R.",13,76.7
"Linda P.",13,80.3
"Ron H.",14,99.1
```

Code Example

```
OPEN "c:\cities.dat" FOR OUTPUT AS #1
WRITE #1, "Cairo", 15000000&  ' Long integers
WRITE #1, "Tulsa", 420500&
WRITE #1, "Auckland", 3000000&
CLOSE #1
```

Code Analysis

This program opens a sequential file named cities.dat on the C: disk drive. The file is a sequential file and is created due to the **FOR OUTPUT** clause of the **OPEN** statement.

The names and populations of three cities are written to the file, and then the file is closed.

The Least You Need to Know

☛ The goal of this chapter is to show you how QBasic stores data on the disk drive in sequential files. A sequential file is easy to create, read, and write. Storing data in a disk file requires that you first open the file. Opening a disk file lets QBasic know the name of the file and also how you want to access the file.

☛ You can access a sequential file in one of three ways: read, write, and append. When you read a file, the data in the file loads from the disk into your program's variables. When you write to a file, the data in your program's variables go to the disk file. When you append to a disk, you add data to data that is already there.

☛ Store data in disk files for long-term storage.

☛ Open all files before you use them, and close them when you are through.

☛ You can create, add to, and read sequential files.

☛ Don't create a sequential file if you ever need to go back and change or reference individual data within the file. Use random-access files for files that change often.

☛ Don't read past the end of a file. Use EOF() so that you'll know when your program reads the last line in a file.

Chapter 21

How Can I Do More with the Disk? Use Random Disk I/O

In This Chapter

- ☞ Creating randomly
- ☞ TYPE your random data first
- ☞ Defining a record variable
- ☞ Working with the File Data
- ☞ Things you can do

A random-access file works just like a big array that is stored on your disk. After you store a random-access file, you can access any line in that file randomly. For instance, you can read a random file backward, read every other line, or change only a little of the file's data without rewriting the entire file, and lots more.

The only requirement of random files is that the data within the files have a uniform appearance. For instance, you wouldn't want to store a lot of text, such as sentences, in random files, but inventory data, people's information, and just about any other kind of

The lines in a random-access file are called *records*. Each line in a random-access file must be of the same format. If the first record has an integer followed by a string followed by a single-precision value, every record in the file also has to have the same format.

data that is duplicated in the same format makes good candidate data for random-access files.

Can you see that there are five records in the data just shown? Each record has four columns. A column in a random-access file is called a *field*. Each field is always a uniform width (therefore, assume that spaces pad the right of the comics' conditions shown here).

Creating Randomly

Suppose you wanted to write a program for your child that kept track of a comic book collection. Your child would want certain information tracked for each comic. He or she would want each comic's title, date, price, and condition stored in the file. Here is a sample of some comic book data that fits this format:

SuperCat	11-09-76 0.25	Fair
Atom Andy	01-22-93 1.25	Good
Hero Harry	07-30-90 0.95	Excellent
Nellie Nurse	08-24-89 0.85	Poor
Computer Thom	12-01-92 1.25	Excellent

Random-access files require a special **OPEN** statement, which takes this format:

OPEN *filename$* FOR RANDOM AS [#]filenumber
LEN=*recordLngth*

The **LEN=***recordLngth* is new to you. A sequential file's records each can be different lengths, so you don't have to specify a record length for sequential files. With random files, you must tell the **OPEN** statement exactly how many memory locations the record takes.

Closing random-access files is no different from closing sequential files. The **CLOSE** for each is the same.

You do not know how to determine the record length of data yet, but the next section shows you a quick way.

TYPE Your Random Data First

Before you can write or read a random-access file, you must describe to QBasic *exactly* how each record will look. In other words, you must define the *record format*. Use the **TYPE** statement to define a random-access file's records. Here is the format of the **TYPE** statement:

TYPE *recordName*
  fieldname AS *type*
  [...*fieldname* AS *type*]
END TYPE

The *recordName* is a name that you give to the format (the look) of the record. The **AS** lines describe each field in the record. The type is one of the values from the table.

Table 21.1   The Type Values for the TYPE Statement

Type	Description
STRING * *n*	A string of n length
INTEGER	Integer
LONG	Long integer
SINGLE	Single-precision
DOUBLE	Double-precision
Type	Another data type you have already defined with another **TYPE** statement

An example **TYPE** statement for the comic book program might look like this:

TYPE comicRec
  title   AS STRING * 15
  comDate   AS STRING * 8
  price   AS SINGLE
  condition AS STRING * 9
END TYPE

Notice that no data type suffixes are needed on the field names. The AS clause describes the field type and eliminates the need for a suffix.

AS STRING specifies the *longest* string length, specified by **STRING * *n*,** you'll need. All string fields must be large enough to accommodate the largest string you'll ever store there.

Remember the **LEN()** function? **LEN()** (as you read in Chapter 12, "Can QBasic Do Much with Strings?") computes and returns the length of the data you put in the parentheses. However, **LEN()** is not just for string data—**LEN()** works on records also. Therefore, at the top of the program that tracked the comic book collection, you would put the previous **TYPE** command, then open the file like this:

OPEN "c:\comics.dat" FOR RANDOM AS #1 LEN=LEN(comicRec)

TYPE only describes the *format* of a record. You still have to define record variables which take on that format.

Defining a Record Variable

One last step is required before you can write to or read from a random-access file. You must define a record variable. Until this point, all your variables were string, integer, long integer, single-precision, or double-precision. A record variable is an *aggregate variable data type*. A record variable is a variable that looks like the record you define with **TYPE**.

An extended form of **DIM** reserves record variables. Here is the format of this new kind of **DIM**:

DIM *recordVar* AS *recordName* [*,..., recordVar* AS *recordName*]

Don't let the keyword **DIM** throw you. Record variables are not arrays. They are variables that take on several data types according to the format of the **TYPE** statement.

The following statement reserves three comic book variables that look like the variables in the figure:

DIM comic1 AS comicRec, comic2 AS comicRec, comic3 AS comicRec

After three record variables have been defined.

What if there are *400* comic books to track? You don't want 400 different variable names. You can dimension an array of record variables. The following statement does just that:

DIM comics(400) AS comicRec ' 400 occurrences of the record

The *dot operator* (which is just a period, .) enables you to store values in specific fields within a record variable. For instance, to store the date 01-22-93 in the date field of **comic2**, you *can't* do this:

comic2 = "01-22-93"   ' INVALID since comic2 is a
' record variable

comic2 is a record variable, not a string variable. To move down to the date field of **comic2**, you *can* do this:

comic2.comDate = "01-22-93"   ' OK

If the comics were stored in an array named **comics**, you could assign the second element a date like this:

comics[2].comDate = "01-22-93"   ' OK

Working with the File Data

After you fill a record variable with values, through assignment, **INPUT**, or **READ-DATA**, you are ready to write the record variable to the disk. The **PUT #** statement writes random records. Here is the format of **PUT**:

PUT [#]*filenumber*, [*recordNumber*,] , *recordVariable*

The opposite of **PUT #** is **GET #**. Often, a mirror-image **GET #** reads data that was written to a file with **PUT #**. Here is the format of **GET #**:

GET [#]*filenumber*, [*recordNumber*,] , *recordVariable*

Typically, one program collects user input and saves it to the file. Another then reports that file's data. Another might enable the user to change one of the file's records (using techniques you'll read about in the next section).

The *recordNumber* is a value that works in the file just the way a subscript works in arrays. For instance, if you wanted to read the 65th record in a file, you could do so this way:

GET #1, 65, comicsBook

If you do not specify a *recordNumber* (it is optional for both **GET #** and **PUT #**), QBasic reads or writes to the record following the last record accessed. You must still include two commas if you do not use a recordNumber in either the **GET #** or the **PUT #**.

The following program asks the user for a comic book's data, then writes (with **PUT**) that data to a random-access file. A series of **GET** statements then reads the file, and **LPRINT** prints the file to the printer.

```
' Program to manage a comic book inventory
TYPE comicRec
    title           AS STRING * 15
    comDate         AS STRING * 8
    price           AS SINGLE
    condition       AS STRING * 9
END TYPE
' Only 1 record variable needed because we'll write just
' as soon as the user fills up the record variable
DIM comic AS comicRec
CLS
PRINT "** C o m i c   B o o k   T r a c k e r **"
PRINT
OPEN "c:\comics.dat" FOR RANDOM AS #1 LEN = LEN(comic)
DO
    PRINT "What is the next comic's title?"
    INPUT "(Press Enter to end the input...) ", Ent$
    IF (Ent$ <> "") THEN
```

```
      comic.title = Ent$
      INPUT "What is the date of the comic"; comic.comDate
      INPUT "What is the price of the comic"; comic.price
      INPUT "What is the comic's condition"; comic.condition
      PRINT
      PUT #1, , comic  ' Puts at the next record
   END IF
LOOP WHILE (Ent$ <> "")
CLOSE #1  ' This close is not really needed since we're going
' to read the same file randomly anyway
' Write a report
LPRINT
LPRINT "Comic Book Inventory"
LPRINT
OPEN "c:\comics.dat" FOR RANDOM AS #1 LEN = LEN(comic)
numRecs = LOF(1) / LEN(comic)
FOR recs = 1 TO numRecs
   GET #1, , comic   ' Read the next record
   LPRINT "Title: "; comic.title
   LPRINT "Date: "; comic.comDate; TAB(20); "Price: ";
   LPRINT USING "#.##"; comic.price
   LPRINT "Condition: ";
comic.condition
   LPRINT
NEXT recs
CLOSE #1
END
```

Things You Can Do

After you understand reading and writing random-access files, you can write more powerful applications. Often, the user wants to change data stored in a random-access file. The change is easy if the user knows the record number. You might do something like this:

OOPS!

You'll notice a strange-looking statement before the **LPRINT** section's **FOR** loop. The **LOF()** function returns the total number of bytes in the file. If you divide that number by the record length of the record variable, you'll get the number of records in the file.

```
INPUT "What is the record number you want to change"; rec
GET #1, rec, comic
' Code to display the data currently in the record
```

Well, this chapter certainly gave you food for thought! You can now write programs that store data in files, then go back into those files as the data changes and update the files.

```
' Let user input new data for the record
PUT #1, rec, comic   ' Write back the new data
```

Of course, how often will the user know the record number of the data to change? Probably rarely or never. Therefore, you have to get more sophisticated. You might have to ask the user for a title (or if this were a business inventory system, you would ask for a part number; or if this were an employee system, you would ask for a Social Security number). Then you could search the file for a title with the code outlined next:

```
DIM ti AS STRING * 15
INPUT "What is the title of the comic you want to change"; ti
' Read through the file looking for the user's title
FOR rec = 1 TO numRecs
   GET #1, rec, comic   ' Read the next record
   IF (comic.title = ti) THEN
      ' Prompt user for new data for this comic
      PUT #1, rec, comic
      EXIT FOR   ' Don't read rest of file
   END IF
NEXT rec
```

Code Example

```
' TV station tracking program
TYPE myTVrec
   channel   AS INTEGER
   station   AS STRING *20
END TYPE
DIM tvVar AS myTVrec   ' Create a record variable
OPEN "c:\tv.dat" FOR RANDOM AS #1 LEN = LEN(tvVar)
FOR i = 1 to 3
   INPUT "What is your favorite channel"; tvVar.channel
   INPUT "What is the name of the station"; tvVar.station
   PUT #1, , tvVar
NEXT i
' Now read the file backward
```

```
PRINT "Here is your list of favorite stations:"
GET #1, 3, tvVar
PRINT "Station: "; tvVar.station; " Channel:"; tvVar.channel
GET #1, 2, tvVar   ' Read second favorite
PRINT "Station: "; tvVar.station; " Channel:"; tvVar.channel
GET #1, 1, tvVar   ' Read top favorite
PRINT "Station: "; tvVar.station; " Channel:"; tvVar.channel
CLOSE #1
END
```

Code Analysis

This program creates a new record named **myTVrec** that contains an integer and a string. A variable is reserved for that record by using a **DIM** statement. (**DIM** reserves arrays, matrices, and record variables.)

A random-access file is then opened, and the user is asked for his or her favorite stations and channels. The data is written to a random-access file and then read back into the program backward before closing the file. There is no way to read a sequential file backwards.

The Least You Need to Know

☛ The goal of this chapter is to extend your knowledge of disk files by showing you how to create, read, and change random-access files. Working with random-access files is some of the most advanced work you can do with QBasic. In contrast to sequential files, you can change data within a random-access file without having to rewrite the entire file.

☛ Reading and writing to random-access files requires that you create records with the **TYPE** command. The **GET** and **PUT** statements then read and write that record data to the random-access disk file that you've opened.

continues

continued

☞ Store data in random-access files if specific data values in the file are subject to change.

☞ Tell QBasic what your file's record looks like with **TYPE**.

☞ Define your record variables with the extended format of **DIM** after you've created the record format with **TYPE**.

☞ Use **GET #** and **PUT #** to read and write data at any location in a random-access file.

☞ Don't use data type suffixes on your **TYPE** field names. The AS clause inside **TYPE** declares the data type.

☞ Don't read past the end of a file. Use **LOF()** as described in this chapter so that you'll know when your program reads the last line in a random-access file.

Chapter 22

What About Long Programs? Organize Them with GOSUB

In This Chapter

- GOSUB-RETURN
- Statement labels
- Why do I need subroutines?

This chapter begins a new direction in your QBasic programming. You now know all the fundamentals of the language. Although there are several commands this book has not covered, most of them are just extensions of the commands you now know. It is time to turn your attention to the future.

Most of your QBasic programs will be longer than the short ones you see here or in any other book on QBasic. Most "real-world" programs are several pages long. As your needs grow, so will your QBasic program size. Before you get too deep, this section of the book will explain how you can better organize your code to make it easier to write and maintain.

The section of code executed by the **GOSUB** statement is called a *subroutine*. A subroutine is a small section within a larger program that executes when you *call* the subroutine with a **GOSUB** statement.⟩

The figure gives you an overview of the GOSUB's purpose. A **RETURN** statement always ends a subroutine's code so that QBasic knows when to get back on the path it was on before GOSUB changed the course.

GOSUB-RETURN

You'll never see a **GOSUB** without a **RETURN** somewhere else in the program. A **GOSUB** is a little like a detour—**GOSUB** overrides the normal flow of a program. Instead of the statement *after* the **GOSUB** executing, a completely different part of the program executes. Eventually, a **RETURN** statement returns the execution to where the **GOSUB** began, and the program continues sequentially from there.

GOSUB causes a program to jump to another location for a while before returning.

Statement Labels

The figure hints at one more item you need to understand before mastering subroutines and **GOSUB**. QBasic has to know exactly where the statements are that you want **GOSUB** to execute. Therefore, you have to label the first statement in the subroutine with a *label* (good name, huh?). A label is a one-word description, from 1 to 40 characters long, that ends with a colon (:). All of these are valid labels:

    Here: **PayCalc:**   **sub1:**   **PrintRoutine:**

Here is the format of GOSUB:

GOSUB *label*

Suppose a subroutine printed your name and address and you wanted to execute that subroutine from various places in a program. Here is an outline of such a program with the full subroutine's code specified:

```
' Outline of a program that calls
' a name and address subroutine
GOSUB nameAddr    ' Calls the subroutine
'
' More statements go here
'
GOSUB nameAddr    ' Calls the subroutine
'
' More statements go here
'
GOSUB nameAddr    ' Calls the subroutine
'
END    ' END keeps QBasic from executing into the subroutine
nameAddr:        ' Label that begins the subroutine
   PRINT "Kay Bryson"
   PRINT "1013 S. Illinois"
   PRINT "Muskogee, OK  74003"
   RETURN
```

BY THE WAY

Notice that the body of the subroutine is indented. The indention helps you distinguish the subroutine from the rest of the program.

The preceding program shows an outline that executes the primary body of the program (the code that would go before the subroutine). The subroutine code labeled **nameAddr:** is called to execute three times because there are three **GOSUB**s in the program. The **END** statement keeps the program execution from "falling through" to the subroutine. Without **END**, QBasic would "fall through" and execute the **PRINT** statements one last time, then would issue an error when the **RETURN** is reached without a corresponding **GOSUB** to get there.

GOSUB subroutine calls are nice to use in **SELECT CASE** statements. Instead of making the **SELECT CASE** contain lots of code, you can keep the **SELECT CASE** short by calling subroutines.

Why Do I Need Subroutines?

If you are asking why you need subroutines, you are right on track. The need for subroutines will become more obvious the more you program and the longer your programs get. As you write long programs, you will find yourself needing to execute the same set of statements several times within a single program. Instead of typing a copy of the code in more than one place, you can stick the code at the bottom of your program, in a subroutine with a label and **RETURN** statement, and then call that code with a **GOSUB** statement when you want the subroutine executed.

Any time your program performs one specific task, such as printing a check or calculating a person's payroll figure, consider putting that code in a subroutine. By using subroutines, you *modularize* your code. The modules, or subroutines, are pieces of the program that are controlled by the GOSUBs above them. If you want to rearrange the program's execution order, you will not have to rearrange code but will only need to rearrange GOSUBs, which are easier to manage.

Not only is your code smaller when you use subroutines (because you don't have to repeat the same lines), but the program is easier to follow later if you need to change or modify it.

Here is a program that displays a menu that asks the user for a certain conversion. A subroutine call performs the conversion desired.

```
' Converts feet to/from meters without subroutines
' There are 39.37 inches in a meter, so there
' are 3.28 feet in a meter
CLS
PRINT "** Conversion **"
DO
  PRINT
  PRINT "Do you want to"
  PRINT "1. Convert meters to feet"
  PRINT "2. Convert feet to meters"
```

```
PRINT "3. Exit the program"
INPUT "What is your choice"; ch
PRINT
SELECT CASE ch
  CASE 1
    GOSUB MetToFeet   ' Call a sub-
routine
  CASE 2
    GOSUB FeetToMet   ' Call a subroutine
  END SELECT
LOOP UNTIL (ch = 3)
END
' Subroutines follow
MetToFeet:
  INPUT "What is the meter value you want converted"; meter
  feet = meter * 3.28
  PRINT "The number of feet in"; meter; "meters is"; feet
  RETURN
FeetToMet:
  INPUT "What is the feet value you want converted"; feet
  meter = feet / 3.28
  PRINT "The number of meters in"; feet; "feet is"; meter
  RETURN
```

If you want to put **END** after the last subroutine in a program, you can, but QBasic does not require it.

Code Example

```
' This is a subroutine that beeps and
' gives the user a warning. This subroutine
' could be called with GOSUB before the
' rest of the program prints on the printer.
prWarn:
  BEEP
  PRINT "Be sure to turn on your printer"
  PRINT "and make sure that it has plenty"
  PRINT "of paper."
  PRINT
  INPUT "Press Enter to continue...", en$
  RETURN
```

Code Analysis

This code shows a subroutine that could be called before the rest of the program prints to the printer (with **LPRINT**). **LPRINT** cannot write to a printer that has no paper or that is not turned on. Instead of the rest of the program warning the user before each **LPRINT**, the rest of the program only has to call the subroutine like this:

GOSUB prWarn

The Least You Need to Know

☞ The goal of this chapter is to show you how to break long programs into more manageable sections called subroutines. The **GOSUB** statements let one part of a program trigger the execution of another part before the first one resumes. Grouping similar statements into their own separate part of the program makes your programs easier to write and test.

☞ Use **GOSUB** to call a subroutine and **RETURN** to make sure that QBasic goes back properly when the subroutine is finished.

☞ Put **END** before the first subroutine's code so that QBasic does not fall through and execute the first subroutine.

☞ Use subroutine calls to keep **SELECT CASE** statements cleaner.

☞ Don't repeat sections of code throughout a program. Put the code in a subroutine and use **GOSUB** to go to the code.

☞ Don't use a colon after a label in a **GOSUB** statement. The colon follows labels only at the *start* of the subroutine, not at the subroutine call.

Chapter 23

Can I Write My Own Functions? No Problem with User-Defined Functions

In This Chapter

- ☛ **DEF FN()** does the trick!
- ☛ A string function example

Remember all those built-in functions that save you so much time? The functions such as **LEFT$()**, **INT()**, and the rest are nice because you don't have to write the code needed to do those jobs. As a matter of fact, the only problem with the built-in functions is that there aren't enough of them. It would be great if you could write your own function and then use that function throughout a program just as if that function were built in.

You *can* write your own functions! These are called *user-defined functions*. You can write string functions or numeric functions. Remember that a function always returns a value. For instance, **MID$()** returns a substring within another string. Also, you pass built-in functions arguments. If you pass **INT()** the argument **13.4**, **INT()** returns **13** (the integer portion of **13.4**).

The functions that you write will receive arguments and return values. Functions are a lot like subroutines. If it weren't for the arguments and return values, a function would be a subroutine.

TECHNO NERD TEACHES...

The concept of a programming language function comes from mathematics. In math, the term *f(x)* is a function that receives an argument *x* and always returns a value based on *x*. That's just what QBasic functions do! As with math functions, you can write QBasic functions that receive more than one argument, but no matter how many arguments you pass, a function can return only one value at a time.

The functions that you write can return only single values, just as the built-in functions do.

DEF FN() Does the Trick!

QBasic's **DEF FN()** statement enables you to define your own functions. After you define a function, the rest of the program can then use that function as if it were a function supplied with the language. Here is the format of **DEF FN()**:

DEF FNname (*arguments*)
  Block of QBasic statements
  FNname = *expression*
END DEF

The data type suffix at the end of the function's name is important. If the function is to return a string, be sure that the function name ends with a **$**. If the function returns a double-precision value, end the function's name with a **#**, and so on.

Remember that the **RND** function returns a random number from **0** to **1**. Also, before calling **RND** (the only numeric function that does not require an argument or parentheses), you need to call **RANDOMIZE TIMER** to truly randomize the **RND** call (I know, it seems silly, but QBasic requires it). Rarely will your programs need a random number from 0 to 1. More likely, you'll need a random number from 1 to another value such as 6 (to simulate a dice roll). You can write your own function that calls **RANDOMIZE TIMER** for you and takes two arguments: the low number and high number of the range of random numbers needed. Here is such a function to clarify things a bit:

```
DEF FNrndRnge (low, high)
   RANDOMIZE TIMER
   rNum = INT(RND * (high - low + 1)) + low
   FNrndRnge = rNum
END DEF
```

The **low** and **high** values are the arguments. In other words, when the program calls this function, two arguments must be specified that indicate the low and high values in the range of random numbers needed. Here is one way you might call this function from somewhere else in the program:

You can probably follow everything in this function until you get to the fourth line. The name of the function, **FNrndRnge**, is being assigned a value! This is the method you use to specify the return value. In other words, the return value of the user-defined function **FNrndRnge** is **rNum**.

rouletteSpin = FNrndRnge(1, 36)

The variable **rouletteSpin** will be assigned the return value of the **FNrndRnge** function. Because a roulette wheel spin can produce a number from 1 to 36 (ruling out **0** and **00**—we're using the European roulette rules here), the function call shown requests a random number from 1 to 36. The function then randomizes the random-number generator via the **RANDOMIZE** statement and then uses the two arguments to convert the random number from 0 to 1 into a number within the range of the **low** to **high** variables (which hold 1 and 36 respectively given the function call shown previously).

Here is a small program that produces some roulette wheel spins:

```
' Program to demonstrate some roulette spins
DEF FNrndRnge (low, high)
   RANDOMIZE TIMER
   rNum = INT(RND * (high - low + 1)) + low
   FNrndRnge = rNum
END DEF
' Actual program begins here
CLS
PRINT "Welcome to the study of roulette!"
PRINT
```

```
PRINT "Here are 30 random spins of a roulette wheel:"
FOR cnt = 1 TO 30
  PRINT FNrndRnge(1, 36);
NEXT cnt
PRINT
PRINT "Would you have bet properly?"
END
```

A String Function Example

Have you heard of the term *palindrome*? A palindrome is a word or phrase spelled the same forward and backward. Here are a couple of the more popular ones:

Race car

Draw pupil's lip upward!

There are several ways to write programs that test for palindromes. One approach is to convert a string to a uniform case (QBasic's built-in UCASE$() function handles that) and then strip the string of its special characters and spaces (you look at only alphabetic characters when testing for palindromes). Using this method would leave compressed phrases like these:

RACECAR

DRAWPUPILSLIPUPWARD

The last step is to reverse the phrase into another string variable and test to see whether the reversed string is equal to the forward string.

Two user-defined string functions will handle the busy work of palindrome testing. Here is a string function that returns an uppercase stripped version of its argument:

```
DEF FNstrip$ (pal$)
  stripStrn$ = ""   ' Start with an empty string
  upPal$ = UCASE$(pal$)
  FOR i = 1 TO LEN(pal$)
```

```
    IF (MID$(upPal$, i, 1) >= "A") AND
    _(MID$(upPal$, i, 1) <= "Z") THEN
       stripStrn$ = stripStrn$ + MID$(upPal$, i, 1)
    END IF
   NEXT i
   FNstrip$ = stripStrn$   ' Return the newly built string
  END DEF
```

Here is a function that returns the reverse of whatever string is passed to it:

```
  DEF FNrev$ (pal$)
    revStr$ = ""    ' Start with a blank string
    FOR i = LEN(pal$) TO 1 STEP -1
                  ' Step back through the string
      revStr$ = revStr$ + MID$(pal$, i, 1)
    NEXT i
    FNrev$ = revStr$
  END DEF
```

After you've entered these two functions, it is very easy to test for palindromes. The following code could appear after the preceding function definitions in a program to tell the user whether the entered word or phrase is a palindrome:

You've never seen a plus sign applied to a string before. The + tacks characters onto the end of a string. **FNstrip$**() adds a character to the new string from the argument if that character is an uppercase letter.

```
  CLS
  INPUT "Please enter a word or phrase...", userPal$
  stripped$ = FNstrip$(userPal$)  ' Strip the user's string
  revUserSt$ = FNrev$(stripped$)  ' Reverse the stripped string
  IF (stripped$ = revUserSt$) THEN
    PRINT "You entered a palindrome!"
  ELSE
    PRINT "You did not type a palindrome."
  END IF
  END
```

Code Example

```
DEF FNareaCir(rad)
   pi = 3.14159
   FNareaCir = pi * rad ^ 2
END DEF
```

Code Analysis

This user-defined function takes one argument, a circle's radius, and computes and returns the area of the circle. The rest of the program could find the area of any circle by calling this function and passing it a radius value such as this line does:

```
PRINT FNareaCir(5)
```

The Least You Need to Know

☛ The goal of this chapter is to show you how to write your own functions that supplement QBasic's built-in functions. Use the **DEF FN** statement to write your functions, and then you can call by name the function that you write.

☛ Functions differ from subroutines because functions always return values. A function can return a single value, and you can then use that return value, either a string or a number, in a QBasic statement or expression.

☛ Write a user-defined function if you want to simulate a built-in function call.

☛ Use the **DEF FN** statement to define your own functions.

☛ Put the data type suffix of the function's return value after the function name that you define.

☛ Don't forget to assign the return value to the function's name inside the user-defined function.

Chapter 24

Can I Separate My Subroutines Further? Use Subroutine Procedures

In This Chapter

- ☛ Specifying subroutine procedures
- ☛ Learn it by trying it
- ☛ Getting around

If subroutines and user-defined functions are good (and they are), *subroutine procedures* are really good! Subroutine procedures were not available with versions of BASIC prior to QBasic. Bringing subroutine procedures into the language makes QBasic able to compete with the "big guys," such as Pascal, C, and FORTRAN.

A subroutine procedure is a subroutine that is completely separated from the rest of the program. A QBasic program that contains one or more subroutine procedures is stored in one program file on the disk when you save it with **File Save**. However, as long as the program is loaded in the QBasic editor, you'll work with the program in pieces, never being able to see the subroutine procedure at the same time as you see any of the rest of the program.

Specifying Subroutine Procedures

The primary difference between a subroutine and a subroutine procedure is that a subroutine is called with **GOSUB** and has a label at the beginning and **RETURN** at the end. A subroutine procedure is called by the **CALL** statement, begins with **SUB**, and ends with an **END SUB** statement. Here is the format of a subroutine procedure:

> **SUB** *procedureName*
>   *One or more QBasic statements*
> **END SUB**

Here is the format of **CALL**:

> **CALL** *procedureName*

When you added subroutines to your programs in Chapter 22 ("What About Long Programs?"), the subroutines went at the bottom of the program, and you could see both the program and the subroutines on-screen at the same time. Now, you won't be able to see them at the same time because QBasic wants you to think of subroutine procedures as though they are a completely different section of the program.

A subroutine procedure is really just a subroutine, but it is a subroutine that is designated by a special **SUB** keyword and that is edited in a different section of QBasic from the rest of the program.

Learn It by Trying It

There is no way to describe QBasic procedures adequately without walking you through a short example. You have to see for yourself what QBasic does when you begin writing code for a subroutine procedure. As you read this section, keep this in mind: A subroutine procedure is *just* a subroutine. However, unlike with the subroutines you read about in Chapter 22, QBasic completely separates subroutine procedures from the rest of your program.

At the end of the preceding chapter, you saw how to write a palindrome program using user-defined functions. The user-defined string functions shown in that program are fine, but those same routines make good subroutine procedure candidates as well. Therefore, this chapter shows you the same program modified so that its palindrome checking is done inside subroutine procedures.

The following section of a program contains two calls to subroutine procedures. Type this program into QBasic.

```
' Program with two subroutine procedures
CLS
INPUT "Please enter a word or phrase...", userPal$

' The subroutine procedure calls follow
CALL stripIt(userPal$)
' Strip the string of special characters
stripped$ = userPal$     ' Save before reversing the string
CALL reverseIt(userPal$)  ' Reverse the contents of the string

' If the pre-reversed string is equal to the reversed string,
' a palindrome was typed
IF (stripped$ = userPal$) THEN   ' If
    PRINT "You entered a palindrome!"
ELSE
    PRINT "You did not type a palin-
drome."
END IF
END
```

You now must include the code that does the work of stripping and reversing the string. We'll do that in two separate subroutine procedures. To see how QBasic handles subroutine procedures, move the cursor to a line or two below the **END** statement, and type this first line of the first subroutine procedure:

SUB stripIt(userPal$)

The variable **userPal$** is the subroutine procedure's argument. As with functions, you can pass one or more arguments to a QBasic subroutine procedure. The procedure can then change those arguments.

CALL is to a subroutine procedure what GOSUB is to a subroutine.

Subroutine procedures never contain RETURN statements. When the subroutine procedure ends, QBasic knows to return the program control to the calling portion of the program.

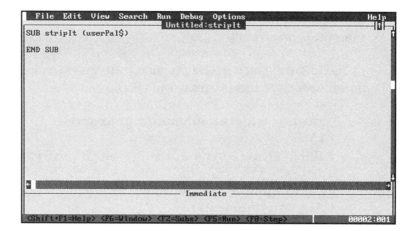

QBasic takes control of the situation when you type a SUB statement.

Did you see what QBasic did? The figure shows your screen at this point. QBasic got rid of all the code except for the **SUB** statement. Then QBasic added an **END SUB** at the end of the subroutine procedure (because all subroutine procedures need an **END SUB**, and QBasic knows it). QBasic is now waiting for you to fill in the body of the subroutine procedure.

TECHNO NERD TEACHES...

QBasic hides all data values inside a subroutine procedure from the calling code. If you want a value in the calling code to be worked on by a subroutine procedure, you must pass that value inside the parentheses as shown in this example, and the **SUB** statement must list the argument as done here as well.

Insert the following code between the **SUB** and the **END SUB** statements. The code is just like the **FNstrip$** function code you saw near the end of the preceding chapter, except that the passed string is modified so that the calling code can work with the modified string.

```
stripStrn$ = ""          ' Start with an empty string
upPal$ = UCASE$(userPal$)   ' Convert passed string to upper
FOR i = 1 TO LEN(userPal$)
  IF (MID$(upPal$, i, 1) >= "A") AND
```

→(MID$(upPal$, i, 1) <= "Z") THEN
   stripStrn$ = stripStrn$ + MID$(upPal$, i, 1)
END IF
NEXT i
userPal$ = stripStrn$ ' Change the argument so the calling
    ' code's userPal$ is now stripped of special characters

It is now time to type the second subroutine procedure. Place the cursor below the **END SUB** statement and type this:

The calling routine is called the *main module*. You first typed a main module, and then the SUB stripIt(userPal$) statement made QBasic open a new subroutine procedure for you to type.

SUB reverseIt(userPal$)

As it always does, QBasic opens up a new editing window for the **reverseIt()** subroutine procedure and enables you to enter that procedure's code. Type the following code between the **SUB** and the **END SUB** statements:

revStr$ = ""   ' Start with a blank string
FOR i = LEN(userPal$) TO 1 STEP -1
' Step back through the string
  revStr$ = revStr$ + MID$(userPal$, i, 1)
NEXT i
userPal$ = revStr$ ' Reverse the string so the main
    ' module can work with the reversed string

If you save the program, QBasic adds the following statements to the top of the main module, whether or not you want it to:

DECLARE SUB stripIt(userPal$)
DECLARE SUB reverseIt(userPal$)

You are now done with one complete program that contains two subroutine procedures. Run the program a few times to see how the subroutine procedures perform the palindrome test. Use these palindromes to test the program:

Faced decaf

Fled a mad elf

QBasic wants these lines (you could have typed them yourself, but why do so when QBasic will do it for you?) at the top of any program with subroutine procedures.

When you save the program or print a listing with File Print, QBasic saves and displays the entire program with subroutine procedures and all. In the QBasic editing window, however, QBasic ensures that you can work with only one procedure or the main module at a time.

Getting Around

You might want to move back and forth between subroutine procedures and the main module as you write programs that use subroutine procedures. The F2 key is the shortcut key to jump back and forth between subroutine procedures and the main module. Press **F2** now and you'll see a list of three items: the main module, the **reverseIt** subroutine procedure, and the **stripIt** subroutine procedure.

You can press the **arrow** keys and press **Enter** or else click with the mouse to choose which one of the three procedures you want to edit next. Therefore, if you are in the **reverseIt** subroutine procedure and want to edit code in the **stripIt** procedure, press **F2** and select the **stripIt** procedure.

Code Example

```
DECLARE SUB encode (wrd$)
' Ask the user for a word to encode
INPUT "What word do you want to encode"; wrd$
CALL encode(wrd$)
END

SUB encode (wrd$)
  s$ = ""
  FOR i = 1 TO LEN(wrd$)
    s$ = s$ + CHR$(ASC(MID$(wrd$, i, 1)) + 1)
  NEXT i
  PRINT s$
END SUB
```

Code Analysis

This program contains a subroutine procedure that receives a string variable and encodes the string by adding 1 to the ASCII value of each letter. The subroutine procedure then converts that ASCII value back to a character and stores the character in a new string named **s$**.

Run this program and look at the encoded value for *HAL.*

The Least You Need to Know

☞ The goal of this chapter is to show you how to make subroutines even more powerful by putting them into subroutine procedures. Subroutine procedures are physically separated from your programs. QBasic separates the variables used in the procedures, so you must pass the variables to the subroutine procedures, whereas you don't have to pass variables to **GOSUB** subroutines.

☞ Use subroutine procedures to really separate subroutines from the main module that called them.

☞ Pass the variables you need to share among subroutine procedures inside parentheses just as you do with function arguments that you pass.

☞ Press **F2** to jump from subroutine procedure to subroutine procedure.

☞ Don't call subroutine procedures with **GOSUB**—use **CALL** instead.

☞ Don't place a **RETURN** at the end of a subroutine procedure. **END SUB** is all you need.

This page unintentionally left blank.

Will QBasic Produce Sounds? Make Noise with QBasic

In This Chapter

- Listening to **SOUND**
- Looking at **SOUND**

Let the fun begin! QBasic programming is not all work—you can have fun as well. This chapter takes up where **BEEP** left off. Rather than a single tone, you can play any noise or song through your PC's speaker with the help of QBasic. The **SOUND** command enables you to control the length, number, and tone of notes.

Programming sound with the **SOUND** command is fun, but your PC is capable of producing only one note at a time. Unless you have an add-on sound card and understand the software that goes with it, programming noise is limited, but it beats not being able to produce sound at all.

Listening to SOUND

Without further ado, type in this program and sit back and listen when you run it:

```
' Program that produces nonsense noises
FOR i = 1 TO 3
   SOUND 440, 3
   SOUND 450, 3
```

```
      SOUND 460, 3
NEXT
FOR i = 1 TO 3
   SOUND 840, 3
   SOUND 850, 3
   SOUND 860, 3
NEXT i
FOR i = 1 TO 2
   SOUND 440, 3
   SOUND 450, 3
   SOUND 460, 3
NEXT
SOUND 440, 6
SOUND 490, 6
SOUND 550, 6
SOUND 590, 6
END
```

OK, the author is an *author*, not a *composer!*

Looking at SOUND

The **SOUND** command produces sound through your PC's speaker. Here is the format of **SOUND**:

SOUND *frequency, duration*

The *frequency* determines which note is sounded. The *frequency* value is a number from **32** to **32767**. The higher the *frequency*, the faster the note vibrates and the higher the note sounds.

Humans can rarely hear notes higher than *frequency* values of *20000*.

The *duration* determines how long the note sounds. It takes a *duration* of **18.2** to sound a note for a single second. To sound a note for two seconds, you would specify **36.4** as the *duration*, and so on.

Getting the exact *frequency* of a number is not always easy. You often have to take a guess and then listen to see whether your guess sounds correct. Microsoft, the maker of QBasic, does tell us that a *frequency* of **440** produces the same note as the A below middle C on a piano. If you double that *frequency* to **880**, you'll hear the A above middle C. Continuing to double **440** gets you each octave above, and continuing to halve **440** gets you each octave below the A below middle C.

The figure shows a portion of a piano keyboard, and some frequencies you can use for the A's. You'll have to do your own extrapolation to get the frequencies of the other notes. Most QBasic programmers use **SOUND** to produce special effects instead of for playing tunes.

OOPS!

If you are unfamiliar with music or pianos, don't fret. This discussion is useful to those who need help mapping some frequencies onto specific notes.

| 55 | 110 | 220 | 440 | 880 | 1760 | 3520 | 7040 |

Mapping some frequency values onto a piano keyboard.

The following program plays each of the As shown in the figure for one second.

```
' Sounds out each octave's A for one second each
SOUND 55, 18.2
SOUND 110, 18.2
SOUND 220, 18.2
SOUND 440, 18.2
SOUND 880, 18.2
SOUND 1760, 18.2
SOUND 3520, 18.2
SOUND 7040, 18.2
END
```

To give you an idea of the range of sounds possible, here is a program that sounds each frequency for a small duration and then runs back down the chromatic scale:

```
' Produces all sounds from low to high and low again
CLS
PRINT "Going up, please!"
' Play the notes going up the frequency scale
```

```
FOR freq = 37 TO 20000 STEP 10
   SOUND freq, .25
NEXT freq
' Play the notes going down the frequency scale
PRINT "DOWN, DOwn, down, ..."
FOR freq = 20000 TO 37 STEP -10
   SOUND freq, .25
NEXT freq
END
```

If you don't have a color monitor, get rid of the **COLOR** statement.

A **STEP** value of 10 was used in the program because it takes so long to cycle through every possible frequency.

The next program gives you some more ideas about the special-effect sounds that are possible. Run the program and you'll hear something that sounds like a clash between a space computer battle and a bad dream!

```
COLOR 12, 2
CLS
LOCATE 12, 34
PRINT "Ooohh..."
' Weird effects
FOR i = 1 TO 35
   freq = INT(RND * 2700) + 500
   dur = INT(RND * 3) + 1
   SOUND freq, dur
NEXT i

' Settling down a little!
FOR freq = 750 TO 450 STEP -7
   SOUND freq, 1
   SOUND 800 - freq, 1
NEXT freq
END
```

Code Example

```
SOUND 1000, 4.5
GOSUB pause
SOUND 800, 2
GOSUB pause
SOUND 800, 1.5
GOSUB pause
SOUND 900, 3
GOSUB pause
SOUND 800, 6
GOSUB pause
SOUND 985, 2.5
GOSUB pause
SOUND 1060, 6
END
pause:
   SOUND 24000, 4   ' Cannot hear this!
   RETURN
```

Code Analysis

This program sounds a series of notes that produce the "Shave and a haircut—two bits!" theme. The subroutine seems to produce a staccato-like pause between sounds, but the pause is actually a note playing at frequency 24000, which is too high for the human ear to hear.

The Least You Need to Know

☞ The goal of this chapter is to teach you about the SOUND statement and how you can use SOUND to add sounds and music to your programs. SOUND requires two arguments, a frequency and the duration (in ticks per second).

☞ Add noise with SOUND to really get your user's attention!

continues

continued

☞ Before writing a song with **SOUND**, you need to practice with **SOUND** until you find the frequencies that match the notes you need.

☞ Don't attempt to **SOUND** a frequency lower than 37 or higher than 32767.

Chapter 26
When Can I Draw? Now, with QBasic Graphics

In This Chapter

- Setting the screen with **SCREEN**
- Connect the dots
- Draw lines with **LINE**
- Box it in!
- Going around in circles

While adding sound to your programs, you might as well add some fancy graphics as well! This chapter explores ways that you can draw on the screen. You must have a VGA color monitor and graphics card to make the programs in this chapter and the next chapter work.

If you are unsure which graphics adapter and monitor you have, don't worry! Try one of the programs here. If you see graphics, you have a monitor that is compatible. If not, you will not have harmed anything by trying.

Setting the Screen with SCREEN

Before displaying anything other than text, you must change the mode of your screen with the **SCREEN** command. Here is the format of **SCREEN**:

SCREEN *mode*

The **SCREEN** *mode* values indicate the kind of graphics that you can draw. When in graphics mode—as opposed to text mode, the default (**SCREEN** *mode* 0)—you can draw so many lines and columns of graphics dots. Each dot is called a *pixel* (which means *picture element*). A pixel is the row and column intersection. For **SCREEN** *mode* 1, for example, you can turn on up to 200 rows and 320 columns of graphics pixels.

Although we'll save learning about colors until the next chapter, you'll notice that some **SCREEN** *mode* values enable you to have more colors at one time than others.

You don't have to issue a **CLS** command to clear your graphics screens. Each **SCREEN** statement erases the screen and sets up the screen for the resulting graphics mode needed.

The more rows and columns a **SCREEN** *mode* provides, the better looking your graphics will be. The pixels will be closer together and will provide straighter lines and curvier circles.

Connect the Dots

The most fundamental graphics command you can specify is turning on and off a pixel. The **PSET** command turns on a pixel, and the **PRESET** command turns off a pixel. Here are the formats of the **PSET** and **PRESET** commands:

PSET [STEP] (*col, row*)

and

PRESET [STEP] (*col, row*)

The minimum *col* and *row* values you can specify are both **0**. The maximum *row* and *col* values are determined by the **SCREEN** *mode* you have set. For example, if you have specified **SCREEN 12**, the maximum **row** value is **479** (there are 480 total rows, and the first one begins at **0**), and the maximum **col** value is **639**.

If you run this short program, you'll have to look closely to see the three dots. **SCREEN** *mode* 12 is a high *resolution* (a fancy name for the density of graphics rows and columns), and the three pixels are small.

You can print text while displaying a graphics screen using **PRINT**, just as you do on a text screen.

To set the screen in a graphics mode and turn on three dots, you can do this:

```
SCREEN 12        ' You must have VGA for this
PSET (100, 100)  ' 101st column and the 101st row
PSET (25, 210)   ' 26th column and the 211th row
PSET (201, 315)  ' 202nd column and the 316th row
```

The **STEP** option of the **PSET** command (and its mirror-image **PRESET** command) lightens your work a little if you have to draw several pixels close together. **STEP** indicates a *relative placement* of the new dots on-screen, compared to the dots you previously drew with **PSET**. For example, to draw a straight line of four pixels, you can do this:

```
SCREEN 12        ' You must have VGA for this
PSET (100, 100)
PSET (100, 101)
PSET (100, 102)
PSET (100, 103)
```

You can also use **STEP** in the last three commands. The *row* and *col* values of **STEP** indicate how far away from the preceding **PSET** you want dots drawn.

```
SCREEN 12        ' You must have VGA for this
PSET (100, 100)
PSET STEP(0, 1)
PSET STEP(0, 1)
PSET STEP(0, 1)
```

PRESET does the opposite of **PSET**. **PRESET** turns off a pixel at the specified *row* and *col* value. The following statements turn off the four pixels just drawn. Notice that last statement uses **STEP** for relative placement of the last turned-off pixel.

The first graphics-oriented commercial video game was called PONG. A simple (by today's standards) video tennis game, PONG started the video arcade craze that began in the late 1970s.

PRESET (100, 100)
PRESET (100, 101)
PRESET (100, 102)
PRESET STEP(0, 1)

Draw Lines with LINE

You can draw lines with **PSET**, but it takes a lot of typing and is slow. The QBasic **LINE** command draws lines quickly and easily. Here is the format of **LINE**:

LINE [STEP] (*col, row*) - [STEP] (*col, row*)

As with **PSET**, you can use **STEP** on subsequent **LINE** commands to draw another line starting next to the place where the preceding line left off.

A line is determined by two end points. Therefore, **LINE** requires that you specify two column and row intersection pairs (the **PSET** requires only one pair). QBasic then draws a line between those points. The following **LINE** statement draws a line from the upper-left screen pixel to the lower-right screen pixel:

LINE (0, 0)-(639, 479)   ' **Draws a diagonal line**

Box It In!

It's easy to turn the **LINE** line-drawing command into a box-drawing command. Add , , **B** to any **LINE** command and QBasic draws a box. As with a line, a box can be drawn from only two row and column pairs (indicating the placement of the upper left corner and the lower right corner of the box).

Here is a statement that draws a box at the top of your screen (assuming that a **SCREEN 12** statement has been issued):

LINE (50, 50)-(600, 225), , B

If you're wondering why the extra comma is needed, a color value will go there in the next chapter. For now, concentrate on drawing the box, and leave the blank between the two commas.

Going Around in Circles

Without a circle, QBasic's drawing commands would stink! As always, QBasic comes to the rescue with a **CIRCLE** command. A circle is known by the location of its center point (an imaginary pixel in the center of the circle you want to draw) and its radius size in pixels. The radius of a circle is the length (in pixels) from its center point to an outer edge. A circle's diameter, or measurement from side to opposite side, is two times the radius value.

You *could* draw a box with four **LINE** statements, but why bother when QBasic can draw the box for you?

Here is the format of the **CIRCLE** command:

CIRCLE [STEP] (*col, row*), *radius*

The *col* and *row* values indicate where the center of the circle will be placed on the screen. The *radius* value indicates the number of pixels in the circle's radius. Here is a command that draws a circle in the center of the screen that has a radius of 50 pixels:

CIRCLE (320, 240), 50

The following program draws lots of circles on your computer's screen. The **RND** function makes sure that each circle's location and radius are different.

```
SCREEN 12
FOR cnt = 1 TO 50          ' Draws 50 circles
   centerCol = INT(RND * 639) + 1 ' From 0 to 639
   centerRow = INT(RND * 479) + 1 ' From 0 to 479
   radius = INT(RND * 100) + 1    ' From 0 to 100
   CIRCLE (centerCol, centerRow), radius
NEXT cnt
END
```

Code Example

```
SCREEN 12
LINE (1, 1)-(479, 639)
```

```
LINE (50, 50)-(200, 200), , B
CIRCLE (320, 240), 40
END
```

Code Analysis

These lines of code draw a line, a box, and a circle on-screen after first setting the video mode to a VGA graphics mode.

The Least You Need to Know

☞ The goal of this chapter is to show you how to draw dots, lines, and circles on your screen. Graphics help produce user interest in your programs, and they certainly make your programs much more fun to use.

☞ When you draw on-screen, you control a series of pixels (meaning picture elements) which are either on or off. The **PSET** and **PRESET** commands turn pixels on and off. The **LINE** command draws lines and boxes, and the **CIRCLE** command draws circles.

☞ Play around with the graphics commands shown in this chapter. That's the only way you'll learn them. Many people feel that the graphics commands are difficult because they appear in the back of books (like this one) rather than up with the "easier" stuff. Not true! QBasic makes graphics easy.

☞ Use the **PSET** command to turn on individual pixels. Use **PRESET** to turn off individual pixels. **LINE** draws both lines and boxes, and **CIRCLE** draws circles.

☞ Don't attempt to specify a **SCREEN** mode value that your graphics adapter and monitor cannot support.

Chapter 27

Is Black and White All I Get? Add Pizzazz with Color

In This Chapter

☞ The colors

☞ Turning on dots in color

☞ Colorful lines

☞ Boxing with colors

☞ Color and **CIRCLE**

☞ Filling in with **PAINT**

If you have a color monitor, there is no good reason to stick to black-and-white graphics! All the graphics commands you learned in the preceding chapter work in different colors. The **SCREEN** mode you specify determines how many colors the *mode* can handle. For instance, this book's tear-out card table of VGA **SCREEN** *mode* values explains that **SCREEN mode 12** supports 16 different colors, and 13 supports up to 256.

This chapter is easy! You only have to add a color option to the graphics commands that you already know.

Some graphics display adapters support more colors (in **SCREEN** *mode* **13**) than the table describes. You'll have to experiment and learn some extended graphics commands (such as **PALETTE**, which is not covered here) if you want to access more than 16 colors at a time.

The Colors

This book's tear-out card contains a color table that you used for the text mode's **COLOR** command way back in Chapter 8, "How Do I Spruce Up My Output?" The colors in the table also work with most of the graphics commands.

Turning On Dots in Color

The **PSET** command turns on white pixels unless you specify a different color (specified in the color value table). **PRESET** also supports color values, but because **PRESET** is used to turn off pixels that are on, the color option isn't used with **PRESET**. To add color to a **PSET** pixel, follow **PSET** with a color value. The next statement turns on a red (color value **4**) pixel at column 100, row 100:

```
PSET (100, 100), 4
```

Color graphics aren't just for games. Many of today's business programs need color to emphasize a point, or just to keep the user's attention. Viewing a colorful screen all day is much more appealing than looking at a drab *monochrome* (one-color) screen.

The following program really makes the point! The program turns on pixels all over the screen in random colors. The **RND** function is used for both the color selection and the row and column positions.

```
SCREEN 12
RANDOMIZE TIMER
FOR dots = 1 TO 1500      ' 1500 dots all together
    colr = INT(RND * 16)   ' A color from 0 to 15
    row = INT(RND * 480)    ' A row from 0 to 479
    col = INT(RND * 640)    ' A column from 0 to 639
    PSET (col, row), colr   ' Turns on the pixel
NEXT dots
END
```

Colorful Lines

Add a color to the **LINE** command just as you did with **PSET** to draw colorful lines on-screen. Here is the format of **LINE** with the color option added:

> LINE (*col, row*), *color*

The following **LINE** command draws a green line diagonally down the screen:

> LINE (0, 0)-(639, 479), 2   ' **Draws a green diagonal line**

Be careful not to go outside your screen's boundaries. If you attempt to draw a line at column **1000** and row **1000**, QBasic draws a line on the side of your monitor, and you'll have to use an eraser to get rid of it. (Just kidding! QBasic ignores your graphics-drawing request if you try to draw further than your screen row and column limits allow.)

Boxing with Colors

Drawing colorful boxes is just as easy as drawing colorful lines. Here is the format of the box-drawing **LINE** command with the color option:

> LINE (*col, row*), *color*, B

The following program draws a bunch of boxes within boxes, each a different color. The figure shows what the screen looks like. The **FOR** loop ensures that 15 boxes (one for every color except black) are drawn.

Resist the temptation to use color as the name of a variable. Remember that **COLOR** is a command name, and you cannot assign names to variables that match the names of commands.

```
SCREEN 12
' Pretty box-drawings
begX = 0
begY = 0
endX = 639
endY = 479
```

```
FOR colr = 1 TO 15    ' Cycles through the colors
   LINE (begX, begY)-(endX, endY), colr, B
   ' Next, adjust the row and column pairs for the next box
   begX = begX + 15
   begY = begY + 15
   endX = endX - 15
   endY = endY - 15
NEXT colr
END
```

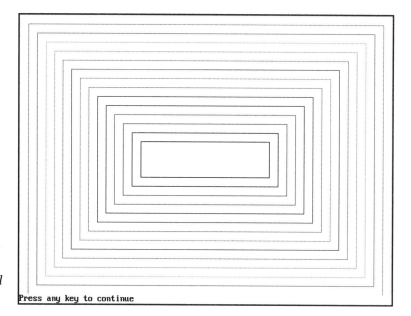

Gosh, those colorful boxes are pretty!

Press any key to continue

Color and CIRCLE

You guessed it . . . the **COLOR** statement also contains a color option. Here is the format of the **CIRCLE** command with a color value:

CIRCLE (*col, row*), *radius, color*

The following program draws a bunch of circles in random colors all over the screen:

```
SCREEN 12
RANDOMIZE TIMER
FOR cnt = 1 TO 150          ' Draws 150 circles
   centerCol = INT(RND * 639) + 1 '
From 0 to 639
   centerRow = INT(RND * 479) + 1 '
From 0 to 479
   colr = INT(RND * 16)          ' From 1
to 15
   radius = INT(RND * 100) + 1    ' From
0 to 100
   CIRCLE (centerCol, centerRow),
radius, colr
NEXT cnt
END
```

Run this program; its effect is interesting.

Paint only fully enclosed shapes. If a shape is not fully enclosed (such as a box with only three sides), the painted color overflows the shape and fills the rest of the screen (or until it runs up against the *borderColor* somewhere).

Filling In with PAINT

The **PAINT** command works just like a can of paint would work if you poured the paint into a glass jar: The paint would fill every nook and cranny of the jar, coloring the sides. After drawing a shape on the screen, use **PAINT** to fill that shape with color, just as if you'd poured paint into the shape. Here is the format of **PAINT**:

> PAINT (*col, row*) [, [*interiorColor*], [*borderColor*]]

After you draw a shape on the screen, the **PAINT**'s *col* and *row* coordinates have to fall somewhere (anywhere) within that shape for **PAINT** to color the entire area with the *interiorColor* value. (If you don't specify an interior color, QBasic uses white.) The *borderColor* tells **PAINT** where to stop painting. The *borderColor* must be the same color as the outline of the shape being filled.

The slot-machine game in Chapter 29 uses **PAINT** to fill in the interior colors for the spinning slot's pictures.

Code Example

```
SCREEN 12
FOR colr = 0 TO 15
   col = INT(RND * 279) + 1
   row = INT(RND * 439) + 1
   LINE (col, row)-(col + 200, row + 200), colr
NEXT colr
```

Code Analysis

This program produces lines randomly on-screen in each of the 16 colors.

The Least You Need to Know

☛ The goal of this chapter is to show you how to produce color graphics. Adding color to your graphics is extremely easy after you've mastered the graphics commands from the preceding chapter. Adding color requires no more than adding a numeric color value to the commands.

☛ Add a color value to any of the graphics commands to spice up your graphics.

☛ Don't use the color option on **PRESET** unless you want to turn *on* a color with **PRESET**. Most QBasic programmers leave the color pixels to **PSET** and reserve **PRESET** for turning off pixels.

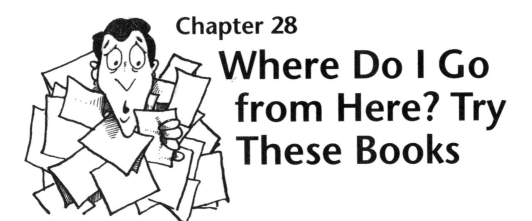

Chapter 28

Where Do I Go from Here? Try These Books

This chapter lists some books that you might want to read now that you know QBasic. Some of the books are beginning-level books for other programming languages that you might be interested in learning. All are from Sams Publishing, and you can order them by calling 1-800-428-5331.

QBasic Programming 101

Readers take an active approach to learning QBasic in this step-by-step tutorial/workbook. Special features such as Find the Bug, Try This, Think About, Finish the Program, and Still Confused? give the reader a thorough understanding of the language. This book discusses QBasic's **PLAY** and graphics features. (For beginning users.)

Teach Yourself QBasic in 21 Days

Users can achieve QBasic success now! Each lesson can be completed in two to three hours or less. Shaded syntax boxes, Q & A sections, and "Do's and Don'ts" sections reinforce the important topics within QBasic. (For beginning to intermediate users.)

Teach Yourself C in 21 Days

With this best-selling book, users can achieve C success now! Each lesson can be completed in two to three hours or less. Shaded syntax boxes, Q & A sections, and "Do's and Don'ts" sections reinforce the important topics within C. (For beginning to intermediate users.)

C++ Programming 101

Readers take an active approach to learning C++ in this step-by-step tutorial/workbook. Special features such as Find the Bug, Try This, Think About, Finish the Program, and Still Confused? give the reader a thorough understanding of the language. (For beginning users.)

Turbo C++ Programming 101

Readers take an active approach to learning Turbo C++ in this step-by-step tutorial/workbook. Special features such as Find the Bug, Try This, Think About, Finish the Program, and Still Confused? give the reader a thorough understanding of the language. (For beginning users.)

Turbo Pascal Programming 101

Readers take an active approach to learning Turbo Pascal in this step-by-step tutorial/workbook. Special features such as Find the Bug, Try This, Think About, Finish the Program, and Still Confused? give the reader a thorough understanding of the language. (For beginning users.)

Chapter 29
Having Fun Yet? Try Playing Around with a QBasic Slot-Machine Game

Programming is not all work and no play—and the following slot-machine game proves it! The game provides a long example that you can study as you master QBasic. The game is kept extremely simple; even so, a lot is happening in this program.

As with all well-written programs, this one is commented thoroughly. You will find more and more of the program understandable as you progress through the book.

Numbers appear to the left of many code lines. These are the numbers of the chapters that discuss the concepts used in the line. If a line confuses you, refer to the appropriate chapter.

> **E-Z**
> When you master enough of QBasic to understand the inner workings of the program, you'll want to explore graphics capabilities and add more symbols to the spinning wheels.

```
CH 04     REM ************************************************************
          ' Casino Slot Machine Game
          ' ------------
          '
          ' This program lets you play a simplified computerized slot
          ' machine and keeps track of your winnings and your losses!
          '
```

```
' Many of the concepts of this book are used in this game,
' including graphics and sound to add special effects.
'

' You must have a standard VGA adapter and monitor to run
' this game.
'

' The game was kept simple so as to demonstrate this book's
' concepts without adding too much complexity. As you get
' more comfortable with QBasic programming, you'll want to
' add more features!
'

' Suggested improvements to the game:
'

' 1. Adjust the randomness of the spin so that the lower-
'    paying combination (three bars) appears more often than
'    3 plums and cherries.
' 2. Add more symbols that don't pay but affect the odds
'    even further.
'
'
```

CH 24
```
DECLARE SUB doWinSound ()
DECLARE SUB finalSpin (totalCash!)
DECLARE SUB spinReels ()
DECLARE SUB drawCherry (colPos%, rowPos%)
DECLARE SUB drawPlum (colPos%, rowPos%)
DECLARE SUB drawBar (colPos%, rowPos%)
```

CH 22
```
GOSUB titleScreen   ' Print opening screen
GOSUB getBetAmt     ' Get amount of money that user has
```

CH 15
CH 05
CH 08
```
DO WHILE (totalCash > 0)
  PRINT
  PRINT USING "&$$###,.##"; "You have:"; totalCash; " to
    ➥bet."
  PRINT "Press Enter to drop a quarter and pull the
    ➥handle..."
```

CH 07	INPUT "(Enter STOP to quit the game)"; ent$
CH 12	IF (UCASE$(LEFT$(ent$, 1)) = "S") THEN
	EXIT DO
CH 13	END IF
CH 22	GOSUB setUpNewGame ' Initialize totals and so forth
CH 24	CALL spinReels ' Go through a cycle of random spins
	CALL finalSpin(totalCash) ' Print last and fixed spin
	' position and update total cash
	' depending on result of the
	' final spin.
CH 15	LOOP
CH 05	CLS
CH 22	GOSUB finalMessage
	END

```
'*************************************************************
titleScreen:
```

CH 04	' This subroutine executes once for the program
CH 26	SCREEN 9
CH 08	COLOR 15, 1
CH 05	PRINT "C a s i n o A c t i o n ! ! !"
	PRINT "---------------"
	PRINT
	PRINT "Welcome to the slot game of the century!"
	PRINT
	PRINT "This game lets you continue playing until you are"
	PRINT "ready to stop or until you run out of money."
	PRINT
	PRINT "Each spin costs you a quarter. Here are the pay-
	offs:"
	PRINT
	PRINT "3 bars: 2.00"

```
CH 24       CALL drawBar(140, 130)
            CALL drawBar(270, 130)
            CALL drawBar(400, 130)
CH 05       PRINT
            PRINT
CH 08       COLOR 15, 1
            PRINT "3 plums: 2.50"
            PRINT
            PRINT
CH 24       CALL drawPlum(140, 170)
            CALL drawPlum(270, 170)
            CALL drawPlum(400, 170)
CH 08       COLOR 15, 1
            PRINT "3 cherries: 3.00"
            PRINT
CH 24       CALL drawCherry(140, 220)
            CALL drawCherry(270, 220)
            CALL drawCherry(400, 220)
CH 22       RETURN


            '***************************************************************


            getBetAmt:

CH 04       ' This subroutine gets the amount of the user's bet in quarters
CH 05          PRINT "Remember, this is only a game. No wagering for real"
               PRINT "(unless you want a chance to win a LOT of CASHola!)"

               PRINT

CH 07       INPUT "How many quarters do you have to bet"; quarters
CH 06       totalCash = quarters * .25
CH 22       RETURN


            '***************************************************************


            setUpNewGame:
CH 11       RANDOMIZE TIMER
CH 06          totalCash = totalCash - .25   ' Each spin costs a quarter
```

```
                  numBars = 0
                  numPlums = 0
                  numCherries = 0
CH 22             RETURN
                finalMessage:
CH 13             IF (totalCash <= 0) THEN
CH 05               PRINT "Too bad. Hope you have a ticket home."
                    PRINT "Come back when you've got more money."
CH 13             ELSE
CH 05               PRINT "You are leaving with money, which is more than"
                    PRINT "I can say for a lot of people!  Good-bye!"
CH 13             END IF
CH 22             RETURN
                END


CH 24           SUB doWinSound
CH 04           ' Generates a rising sound for a winning combination
CH 16             FOR tone = 1000 TO 10000 STEP 450
CH 25                 SOUND tone, 1
                    NEXT tone
CH 24           END SUB


CH 24           SUB drawBar (colPos%, rowPos%)
CH 04           ' Draws a yellow bar

CH 26             LINE (colPos%, rowPos%)-(colPos% + 80, rowPos% + 30), 14, B
CH 27             PAINT (colPos% + 1, rowPos% + 1), 14, 14
CH 08             COLOR 15, 1 ' Reset screen to white letters, blue background
CH 24           END SUB



CH 24           SUB drawCherry (colPos%, rowPos%)
CH 04           ' Draws a cherry with a stem
                ' Adjust for cherry's shape
CH 10             colPos% = colPos% + 35
                  rowPos% = rowPos% + 10
                ' cherry outline
CH 26             CIRCLE (colPos%, rowPos%), 6, 4
                  CIRCLE (colPos% - 7, rowPos% + 3), 6, 4
                  CIRCLE (colPos% - 1, rowPos% + 6), 6, 4
                ' red color
```

```
CH 27        PAINT (colPos% + 1, rowPos%), 4, 4
             PAINT (colPos% - 7, rowPos% + 3), 4, 4
             PAINT (colPos%, rowPos% + 6), 4, 4
             ' stem

CH 26        LINE (colPos%,rowPos% + 2)-(colPos% + 20,rowPos% + 4), 4, B
CH 27        PAINT (colPos% + 19, rowPos% + 3), 2, 4
CH 24      END SUB


CH 24        SUB drawPlum (colPos%, rowPos%)
CH 04        ' Draws a purple plum
             ' Adjust for plum shape
CH 10          colPos% = colPos% + 20
               rowPos% = rowPos% + 20

CH 26        CIRCLE (colPos% + 19, rowPos% - 5), 18, 13
CH 27        PAINT (colPos% + 19, rowPos% - 5), 13, 13
CH 26        LINE (colPos% + 37, rowPos%)-(colPos% + 39, rowPos% + 2), 6
CH 26        PSET (colPos% + 19, rowPos% - 9), 0
             PSET (colPos% + 24, rowPos% - 8), 0
             PSET (colPos% + 27, rowPos% - 6), 0
             PSET (colPos% + 25, rowPos% - 4), 0
CH 24      END SUB


CH 24        SUB finalSpin (totalCash)
CH 04        ' Generates a final spin and adds to total if a winning
             ' combination

CH 05          CLS
CH 08          COLOR 15, 1
CH 16          FOR i = 1 TO 3
CH 11          n = INT(3 * RND) + 1
CH 14          SELECT CASE n
                 CASE 1
CH 24              CALL drawBar(i * 130, 130)
                   numBars = numBars + 1
                 CASE 2
```

```
CH 24          CALL drawPlum(i * 130, 130)
               numPlums = numPlums + 1
             CASE 3
CH 24          CALL drawCherry(i * 130, 130)
               numCherries = numCherries + 1
             END SELECT
             NEXT i
CH 13        IF numBars = 3 THEN          ' 3 bars printed
CH 24          CALL doWinSound
CH 05          PRINT "Three bars!  You Win $2.00!!"
CH 10          totalCash = totalCash + 2!
CH 13        ELSEIF numPlums = 3 THEN        ' 3 plums printed
CH 24          CALL doWinSound
CH 05          PRINT "Three plums!  You Win $2.50!!"
CH 06          totalCash = totalCash + 2.5
CH 13        ELSEIF numCherries = 3 THEN   ' 3 cherries printed
CH 24          CALL doWinSound
CH 05          PRINT "Three cherries!  You Win $3.00!!"
CH 10          totalCash = totalCash + 3!
CH 13        END IF

CH 24        END SUB

CH 24        SUB spinReels
CH 16        FOR spin = 1 TO 3
CH 24          CALL drawPlum(130, 130)
               CALL drawCherry(260, 130)
               CALL drawBar(390, 130)
CH 25          SOUND INT(RND * 8000) + 37, 1.82
CH 05          CLS
CH 08          COLOR 15, 1
CH 24          CALL drawPlum(390, 130)
               CALL drawCherry(130, 130)
               CALL drawBar(260, 130)
CH 25          SOUND INT(RND * 8000) + 37, 1.82
CH 05          CLS
CH 08          COLOR 15, 1
```

CH 24	**CALL drawPlum(260, 130)**
	CALL drawCherry(390, 130)
	CALL drawBar(130, 130)
CH 25	**SOUND INT(RND * 8000) + 37, 1.82**
CH 05	**CLS**
CH 08	**COLOR 15, 1**
	NEXT spin
CH 24	**END SUB**

Chapter 30
ASCII Chart

Dec	ASCII Character
000	null
001	☺
002	●
003	♥
004	◆
005	♣
006	♠
007	●
008	■
009	○
010	■
011	♂
012	♀
013	♪
014	♪♪
015	☼
016	►

Dec	ASCII Character
017	◄
018	↕
019	‼
020	¶
021	§
022	▬
023	↨
024	↑
025	↓
026	→
027	←
028	FS
029	GS
030	RS
031	US
032	SP
033	!
034	"
035	#
036	$
037	%
038	&
039	'
040	(
041	)
042	*
043	+
044	,
045	-
046	.
047	/

Dec	ASCII Character
048	0
049	1
050	2
051	3
052	4
053	5
054	6
055	7
056	8
057	9
058	:
059	;
060	<
061	=
062	>
063	?
064	@
065	A
066	B
067	C
068	D
069	E
070	F
071	G
072	H
073	I
074	J
075	K
076	L
077	M
078	N

Dec	ASCII Character
079	O
080	P
081	Q
082	R
083	S
084	T
085	U
086	V
087	W
088	X
089	Y
090	Z
091	[
092	\
093	]
094	^
095	_
096	`
097	a
098	b
099	c
100	d
101	e
102	f
103	g
104	h
105	i
106	j
107	k
108	l
109	m

Dec	ASCII Character
110	n
111	o
112	p
113	q
114	r
115	s
116	t
117	u
118	v
119	w
120	x
121	y
122	z
123	{
124	¦
125	}
126	~
127	DEL
128	Ç
129	ü
130	é
131	â
132	ä
133	à
134	å
135	ç
136	ê
137	ë
138	è
139	ï
140	î

Dec	ASCII Character
141	ì
142	Ä
143	Å
144	É
145	æ
146	Æ
147	ô
148	ö
149	ò
150	û
151	ù
152	ÿ
153	Ö
154	Ü
155	¢
156	£
157	¥
158	P$_t$
159	ƒ
160	á
161	í
162	ó
163	ú
164	ñ
165	Ñ
166	a
167	o
168	¿
169	⌐
170	¬
171	½

Dec	ASCII Character
172	¼
173	¡
174	«
175	»
176	░
177	▒
178	▓
179	│
180	┤
181	╡
182	╢
183	╖
184	╕
185	╣
186	║
187	╗
188	╝
189	╜
190	╛
191	┐
192	└
193	┴
194	┬
195	├
196	─
197	┼
198	╞
199	╟
200	╚
201	╔
202	╩

Dec	ASCII Character
203	╦
204	╠
205	=
206	╬
207	╧
208	╨
209	╤
210	╥
211	╙
212	╘
213	╒
214	╓
215	╫
216	╪
217	┘
218	┌
219	█
220	▄
221	▌
222	▐
223	▀
224	α
225	β
226	Γ
227	π
228	Σ
229	σ
230	μ
231	τ
232	Φ
233	θ

Dec	ASCII Character
234	Ω
235	δ
236	∞
237	$\emptyset$
238	$\in$
239	$\cap$
240	$\equiv$
241	$\pm$
242	$\geq$
243	$\leq$
244	$\lceil$
245	$\rfloor$
246	$\div$
247	$\approx$
248	$\circ$
249	•
250	·
251	$\sqrt{}$
252	η
253	2
254	■
255	

NOTE: The last 128 ASCII codes listed in this table, numbers 128 through 255, are specific to IBM PCs and IBM compatibles.

**It's OK—go ahead and write on this page.
You paid for it.**

Index

Who cares what you think? WE DO!

We take our customers' opinions very personally. After all, you're the reason we publish these books. If you're not happy, we're doing something wrong.

We'd appreciate it if you would take the time to drop us a note or fax us a fax. A real person—not a computer—reads every letter we get, and makes sure that your comments get relayed to the appropriate people.

Not sure what to say? Here are some details we'd like to know:

- ☛ Who you are (age, occupation, hobbies, etc.)
- ☛ Where you bought the book
- ☛ Why you picked this book instead of a different one
- ☛ What you liked best about the book
- ☛ What could have been done better
- ☛ Your overall opinion of the book
- ☛ What other topics you would purchase a book on

Mail, e-mail, or fax it to:

Faithe Wempen
Product Development Manager
Alpha Books
201 West 103rd Street
Indianapolis, IN 46290

FAX: (317) 581-4669
CIS: 75430,174

Special Offer!

Alpha Books needs people like you to give opinions about new and existing books. Product testers receive free books in exchange for providing their opinions about them. If you would like to be a product tester, please mention it in your letter, and make sure you include your full name, address, and daytime phone.

Other Idiot-Proof Books from Alpha...

The Complete Idiot's Pocket Guides

Cheaper Than Therapy!

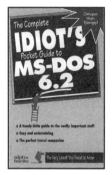

The Complete Idiot's Pocket Guide to MS-DOS 6.2
ISBN: 1-56761-417-5
Softbound

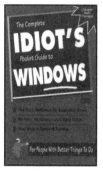

The Complete Idiot's Pocket Guide to Windows
ISBN: 1-56761-302-0
Softbound

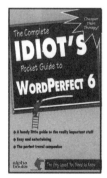

The Complete Idiot's Pocket Guide to WordPerfect 6
ISBN: 1-56761-300-4
Softbound

Also Available!

The Complete Idiot's Pocket Guide to Excel
ISBN: 1-56761-370-5
Softbound

The Complete Idiot's Pocket Guide to WordPerfect for Windows
ISBN: 1-56761-371-3
Softbound

The Complete Idiot's Pocket Guide to Word for Windows 6
ISBN: 1-56761-368-3
Softbound

Also Available!

**The Complete Idiot's Guide
to 1-2-3, New Edition**
ISBN: 1-56761-404-3
Softbound

**The Complete Idiot's Guide to
1-2-3 for Windows**
ISBN: 1-56761-400-0
Softbound

**The Complete Idiot's Guide
to Ami Pro**
ISBN: 1-56761-453-1
Softbound

**The Complete Idiot's Guide to
Buying & Upgrading PCs**
ISBN: 1-56761-274-1
Softbound

**The Complete Idiot's Guide to
Computer Terms**
ISBN: 1-56761-266-0
Softbound

**The Complete Idiot's Guide
to Excel**
ISBN: 1-56761-318-7
Softbound

**The Complete Idiot's Guide
to Internet**
ISBN: 1-56761-414-0
Softbound

**The Complete Idiot's Guide
to The Mac**
ISBN: 1-56761-395-0
Softbound

**The Complete Idiot's Guide
to VCRs**
ISBN: 1-56761-294-6
Softbound

**The Complete Idiot's Guide
to WordPerfect**
ISBN: 1-56761-187-7
Softbound

**The Complete Idiot's Guide to
WordPerfect for Windows**
ISBN: 1-56761-282-2
Softbound

**The Complete Idiot's Guide
to Word for Windows**
ISBN: 1-56761-355-1
Softbound

**The Complete Idiot's Guide
to Works for Windows**
ISBN: 1-56761-451-5
Softbound